RIDER HAGGARD AND THE FICTION OF EMPIRE

While Rider Haggard's stories have been popular with several generations of readers, this is the first study to examine the place of Empire in his writing and to draw out its related political and literary implications. Dr Katz argues that the romance adventure carried an ideological burden for Haggard and that he was one of a number of imperial-minded writers – among them R. L. Stevenson, Andrew Lang, W. E. Henley, and Kipling – who shared a similar world-view and certain literary traits.

The book includes a biographical sketch focusing on Haggard's experiences in the Transvaal in the late 1870s and early 1880s, and his association with South Africa throughout his life; a description of the imperial background, with particular attention paid to the imperial emphasis on leadership and heroism; an analysis of romance as a literary genre; and a detailed study of Haggard's work with reference to that of other imperial writers. Questions of heroism, fatalism, stoicism, anti-materialism, and spiritualism are discussed in terms of their relationship to the imperial ethos, and in a culminating chapter, which contains previously unpublished material from Haggard's diaries, the issue of race and racism is considered. The importance of this last chapter is its placing of racism as a natural 'conclusion' to Empire.

This book will be of value and interest to specialists in literature, imperial history and politics, and related cultural studies, as well as to readers of Haggard.

Portrait of Rider Haggard by William Strang, 1916
(reproduced by kind permission of Commander Mark E. Cheyne)

RIDER HAGGARD AND THE FICTION OF EMPIRE

A critical study of British imperial fiction

WENDY R. KATZ

Associate Professor of English
Saint Mary's University, Halifax, Nova Scotia

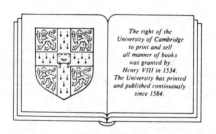

The right of the
University of Cambridge
to print and sell
all manner of books
was granted by
Henry VIII in 1534.
The University has printed
and published continuously
since 1584.

CAMBRIDGE UNIVERSITY PRESS

Cambridge
New York   New Rochelle   Melbourne   Sydney

Published by the Press Syndicate of the University of Cambridge
The Pitt Building, Trumpington Street, Cambridge CB2 1RP
32 East 57th Street, New York, NY 10022, USA
10 Stamford Road, Oakleigh, Melbourne 3166, Australia

First published 1987

Printed in Great Britain at
the University Press, Cambridge

British Library cataloguing in publication data
Katz, Wendy R.
Rider Haggard and the fiction of empire:
a critical study of British imperial fiction.
1. Haggard, H. Rider (Henry Rider) 1856–1925
– Criticism and interpretation
I. Title
823′.8   PR4732

Library of Congress cataloguing in publication data
Katz, Wendy R. (Wendy Roberta), 1945–
Rider Haggard and the fiction of empire.
Bibliography.
Includes index.
1. Haggard, H. Rider (Henry Rider), 1856–1925 –
Political and social views.   2. Colonies in literature.
3. Imperialism in literature.   4. South Africa in
literature.   5. Race relations in literature.
6. Adventure stories, English–History and criticism.
I. Title.
PR4732.K38   1987   823′.8   87–6581

ISBN 0 521 33425 X

wv

CONTENTS

———

ACKNOWLEDGEMENTS

———

I wish to acknowledge my indebtedness to Saint Mary's University for support given to this project through the Senate Research Grants programme. I am particularly grateful to Professor John Fraser, who has been a source of encouragement in this project for many years. I would also like to thank Professor Morton Cohen for a supportive reading of an early draft of this book. My greatest debt is to Alan Young, whose careful reading of the manuscript in its final stages and whose unfailing interest from the start have made this book possible.

For access to material in their libraries I am grateful to: Kenneth A. Lohf, Librarian for Rare Books and Manuscripts, Columbia University; Jean M. Kennedy, County Archivist, Norfolk Record Office; and the librarians at Dalhousie and Saint Mary's universities. Lord Carnarvon's letter appears by permission of Columbia University, H. Rider Haggard Papers, Rare Book and Manuscript Library. Selections from the Haggard Diaries and the William Strang photograph appear by permission of Commander Mark E. Cheyne, Ditchingham House, Norfolk. An early version of chapter 5 appeared in *English Literature in Transition*.

INTRODUCTION

In 1926, when Horace G. Hutchinson reviewed Rider Haggard's autobiography, *The Days of My Life*, he spoke of Haggard's considerable influence on young men in Britain:

it is not to be doubted that [Haggard's] South African romances filled many a young fellow with longing to go into the wide spaces of those lands and see their marvels for himself, and have thus aided far more than we can ever know in bringing British settlers and influence into the new country. They have helped to accomplish the dreams and aims of Rhodes. (p. 344)

It is easy to find supporting evidence for the view that Haggard helped create an image of Empire for the young men of his day and even led some of them into imperial service. Harvey Darton, in his classic *Children's Books in England* (1932), asserted, for example, that Haggard 'gave English boys a better idea of the potential wonders of Empire than could be had from any school task' (1966, p. 304). Almost twenty years later, Graham Greene, who was one of these English boys, speculated nostalgically in his *The Lost Childhood* (1951) on the lingering effects of *King Solomon's Mines*:

If it had not been for that romantic tale of Allan Quatermain, Sir Henry Curtis, Captain Good, and, above all, the ancient witch Gagool, would I at nineteen have studied the appointments list of the Colonial Office and very nearly picked on the Nigerian Navy for a career? And later, when surely I ought to have known better, the old African fixation remained. (p. 14)

In addition to Haggard's power to captivate, Greene said, was his uncommon ability to impart an historical view. 'Far more than Scott', he wrote, 'Haggard gave us a sense of history' (1951, p. 310). Ivor Brown, in a 1961 review of Morton Cohen's *Rider Haggard, His Life and Work* (1960), also admitted to having been one of those children who were bewitched by Haggard's fiction: 'I . . . can remember the exact time and place at which I picked up "King Solomon's Mines" and was enthralled' (p. 45). Moreover, he added, 'There must still be

1

many thousands on whom Haggard's vision of Africa made an immense and enduring impact in childhood' (p. 45).

Haggard's influence was not limited to schoolboy circles. The general public could not help but notice this prominent figure. His letters to the editor of *The Times* on all manner of subjects appeared regularly from 1885 to his death in 1925. A history of South Africa, *Cetywayo and His White Neighbours* (1882), was followed by books on gardening and agriculture: *A Farmer's Year* (1899), *Rural England* (1902), *A Gardener's Year* (1905), and *Rural Denmark* (1911). He wrote two books on the Salvation Army, *The Poor and the Land* (1905) and *Regeneration* (1910), of which the latter won him the praise and friendship of Theodore Roosevelt. During the First World War he proposed a plan for the resettlement of British soldiers in *The After-War Settlement and the Employment of Ex-Service Men in the Overseas Dominions* (1916). All this was in addition to his articles and letters to periodicals, his two-volume autobiography, and his fifty-eight volumes of fiction. Newspapers eagerly reported his comings and goings in conspicuous headlines. Much more than a popular writer, Haggard was a celebrity.

Yet, over the last forty-odd years critics have periodically remarked that Haggard has still not been given his due. Gordon Hall Gerould, in *The Patterns of English and American Fiction* (1942), said that 'Haggard was, after all, a writer of far greater importance than it has been the custom to consider him' (p. 416). A *Times Literary Supplement* reviewer said on 11 April 1958 that, 'On the strength of *King Solomon's Mines* alone he deserves a place higher than that generally reserved for him' ('The wheat and the chaff', p. xxii). C. S. Lewis, who admired Haggard's gift of story-telling, wrote in *Time and Tide*: 'it is no longer any good pretending that his best work was merely an ephemeral and commercial success' (1960, p. 1044). More recently, Haggard's works were praised by Peter Porter, who in his 7 July 1972 'Viewpoint' in *The Times Literary Supplement* pronounced Haggard's *Nada the Lily* 'one of the finest novels of the nineteenth century' (p. 774). In 1978, a biography of Haggard appeared, Peter Berresford Ellis's *H. Rider Haggard, A Voice from the Infinite*, and in 1980, D. S. Higgins's *The Private Diaries of Sir H. Rider Haggard, 1914–1925*, a one-volume distillation of twenty-two manuscript volumes, added a unique wartime and post-war dimension to the picture of Haggard. A year later, Peter Haining edited *The Best Short Stories of Rider*

Haggard, and more was on the way: *Rider Haggard, A Biography* (1983), another offering by Higgins, and *Rider Haggard* (1984), a Twayne series book, by Norman Etherington. Given such unequivocal and persistent attention, it would seem that Rider Haggard's place in literary history is far from settled.

The second edition of Morton Cohen's study of Haggard (1968), with its scrupulous documentation, its appreciative understanding of its subject, and its sober aversion to exaggerated assertions regarding Haggard's significance as a writer, will probably remain the standard work on Haggard for some time. Cohen, however, while not indifferent to Haggard's imperial views, did not attempt to question their manipulative or exploitative features. He took the imperial stance for granted, leaving others with the task of sorting out its workings and its implications.

Alan Sandison turned his hand to the task in a curiously depoliticized analysis of literature and imperialism in *The Wheel of Empire* (1967), a group of essays on Haggard, Kipling, Conrad, and Buchan, exploring the 'nature and function of the imperial idea' (p. vii) in their respective works. Treating each figure as a special case, Sandison suggests that imperialism exists as something quite separate from the creative writer, something outside, to which the writer responds in a distinctly personal way. 'Given the [imperial] idea', he says of Kipling, 'he reacted in the way any artist would – by finding in it a means through which to express his own artistic vision' (p. 195). Kipling's vision, according to Sandison, is the 'awareness of man's essential isolation . . . illuminated in the imperial alien's relationship to his hostile environment' (p. 112). Sandison does not hold imperialism even partially responsible for helping to create isolation or fragmentation; it merely clarifies an already existent situation. As I shall argue later, the Empire appears to be more an intrusive annoyance to Sandison than it is anything else. Sandison thinks it 'unfortunate . . . that Kipling chose the physical context of a political idea' to express his own singular vision, because his support of Empire 'concealed the fact that, fundamentally he was *not* writing to express the idea of empire' (p. 112). With such logic, it is not surprising to find Sandison responding in a similar vein to Haggard's writings and even concluding that Haggard was able to 'escape the vice of racial prejudice' (p. 31), an opinion which results from a remarkable view of the evidence. For Sandison, the Empire is a cumbersome historical burden somewhat arbitrarily grafted atop a unique and apolitical vision.

Any study of Haggard's work that fails to acknowledge its pervasive imperialism falls far short of satisfactory; hence the necessity of stating here that the imperial world was directly related to the world of Haggard's romances. An aggressive political policy and a literature which emphasized physical action were of a piece. It hardly needs saying that the Empire figures significantly in the works of not only Haggard, but writers such as Kipling, Henty, Conan Doyle, John Buchan, and others. South Africa and India were introduced to the British public primarily through the works of these men. But Haggard's romances, in particular, illustrate a total mentality, a philosophy of life, an idea of humankind completely in harmony with the imperial ideology.

Haggard will doubtless always occupy a minor place in the history of literature, but he is, none the less, of considerable cultural significance, as I hope to be able to demonstrate. He was an ideological presence, part of his period's popular culture; and he contributed to a certain state of mind. He assisted in the propagation of imperial ideas and created for Britain an image of greatness and superiority, an image of the world with the British in control. It is in this sense that he is a force to be reckoned with. A dynamic relationship exists between late nineteenth-century imperialism and the literary climate of Great Britain, the development of romance literature being the most striking by-product of this relationship. The interconnecting links can be clarified and made more intelligible by an examination of Haggard and his writings.

Although it is possible to divide Haggard's fiction into three groups – the romances of adventure, the historical romances, and the romances of contemporary life – these divisions are not sufficiently different to warrant separate treatment as such. While the romances of adventure are characterized by their exotic backgrounds and emphasis on action, the historical romances by their reconstruction of the past and stress on particular historical themes, and the romances of contemporary life by the importance of domestic and social situations, they all exhibit enough in common to obviate the necessity of being accorded special categories. *The Way of the Spirit* (1906), for example – nominally a romance of contemporary life because of its Mayfair setting, its family conflicts, its themes of love and marriage, and its focus on British politics – is also set in the Sudan, lays great stress on the imperial heroism of its protagonist, Rupert Ullershaw, and is generally both exotic and activist enough to be treated alongside the works which are more exclusively adventurist. *Jess* (1887) and *Beatrice* (1890), two more works that deal with love and marriage and may be classified as romances of contemporary life, also give prominence to imperial issues, an emphatic heroism, and a deep vein of fatalism which allow them to be placed alongside the romances of adventure. The historical romances, ostensibly different from the two other groups because of their period settings and motifs, none the less possess certain ideas, attitudes and (in the case of the adventure stories) exploits of adventure in common. All three groups alike show the markings of imperial pressure.

Also important is the manner in which the chronological development of Haggard's works indicates the influence exerted by specific political events on the evolution of his consciousness. During the post-Boer War period, for example, Haggard delivered exhortations on military preparedness to British readers in *Ayesha* (1905) and *Queen Sheba's Ring* (1910). Equally revealing are the 'Unionist' qualities in *The Way of the Spirit*, which, along with the earlier works of the eighties such as *Dawn* (1884), *The Witch's Head* (1884), *Jess* (1887), and *Colonel Quaritch, V.C.* (1888), is an anti-Gladstone work. Although the earlier fiction, as one might expect, is more preoccupied with events in South Africa than is the later fiction, an interest in South Africa reappears in the 1912–17 Zulu trilogy, possibly sparked by his work on a Royal Commission the mandate of which included a trip to this African dominion. Yet, in spite of the topical concerns in his works, there is, in the main, little discernible change in Haggard's opinions over the years. His philosophical and political ideas stayed more or less the same, and his appetite for action and adventure continued undiminished. Although his optimism receded towards the end of his life, Haggard remained to the last a firm imperial defender.

Chapter 1

THE DAYS OF HIS LIFE

The world into which Rider Haggard was born in 1856 was one of agricultural prosperity. Despite the repeal of the Corn Laws in 1846, the price of wheat was secure and consumer markets were on the increase. Rents were high, property was still in great demand, and profits were assured beyond question. Haggard warmly recalled this period – the years of his youth – in his autobiography, declaring that 'it would have been difficult to find a more jovial party than we were at Bradenham [his family's estate of about 400 acres in West Norfolk] in the days of my youth' (1926a, I, p. 23). The relative security of the rural world around him at this time stands out in sharp contrast with the rural insecurity he saw as an adult, when prosperity was at an end and agriculture entered an era of depression from which it never fully recovered. With the depression of the late seventies came the exodus to the cities which deprived the land of its labour and the landowner of much of his traditional wealth and power. In spite of the great agrarian upheaval, Haggard's love of the land remained with him throughout his life, for he saw the land as a source of strength and stability, and in this he was, in addition to being a defender of the Empire, an apologist for the dying landowning class. As far as Haggard was concerned, the love of Empire and the love of the land were inseparable, both loves being the principal stimuli for his sense of dynasty.

In 1875 a minor part of the dynastic process that was Empire was set in motion when Haggard's father wrote to Sir Henry Bulwer, the newly appointed Lieutenant-Governor of Natal, enquiring about a place for his son. Since the Bulwers and the Haggards were old family friends, a place was found, and Haggard, at the age of nineteen, started off for South Africa. His duties were mostly managerial at first. He was in charge of hiring servants, ordering food, and arranging for entertaining. Soon he was given the opportunity to explore his new surroundings. In 1876, he went with Bulwer to Chief Pagate's kraal where a war dance was being performed in honour of the Lieutenant-Governor. This he describes in one of his first articles, 'A Zulu War Dance', published in the *Gentleman's Magazine*. Already his response to Africa was keenly romantic, as he demonstrates in his description of the countryside seen on his way to the kraal: 'It was like coming face to face with great primeval Nature, not nature as we civilised people know her, smiling in cornfields, waving in well-ordered woods, but Nature as she was on the morrow of the Creation' (1877a, p. 99).

Haggard quickly became aware of the precarious political situation in South Africa. Boers and blacks were plaguing each other by skirmishes and constant quarrels, and Boers and British were openly exchanging insult for insult. As Joseph Lehmann put it in his *The First Boer War*, 'While the sun never set on the British Empire, the blood never seemed to dry in South Africa. Britons, Boers, and blacks clashed and fought and fought again, in a fashion bewildering to those in distant centres of world civilization' (1972, p. 13). It was shortly after Haggard arrived that the Pedi chief Sekhukhune and the Boers were engaged in skirmishes along the border of the Transvaal, which erupted into a full-scale battle in which the Boers were defeated and their financial and military strength seriously weakened.[1] It was such confusion and turmoil that led to the eventual annexation of the Transvaal by the British. In this Haggard was to play a part.

Haggard arrived in South Africa at the very moment that Britain assumed a more aggressive imperial stance. Disraeli's Colonial Secretary was Lord Carnarvon, the man who had successfully sponsored the British North America Act in 1867 to federate Canada. Carnarvon now wished to do the same for the South African states. With the defeat of the Boers at the hands of Sekhukhune and the ensuing confusion in the Transvaal, the time seemed right. Besides, Cetshwayo, then chief of the Zulus, threatened to invade the Transvaal, and it was thought unlikely that the Boers could repel the Zulu army. The British could thus offer military protection to the Boers as well as financial support. Carnarvon sent Sir Theophilus Shepstone, Secretary for Native Affairs, to the Transvaal to see about the possibility of annexation. On his mission to Burgers's state, Shepstone took Rider Haggard.

According to Haggard, Shepstone conducted a 'champagne and sherry policy' (1926a, I, p. 62) and needed Haggard to look after the entertaining. (It was with Shepstone that Haggard met M'hlopekazi, the Swazi attendant who later stood as a model for the fierce, loyal Umslopogaas, Allan Quatermain's friend.) The trip from Pietermaritzburg taking less than a month, they arrived in July 1877 and, in Haggard's view, were welcomed enthusiastically. Haggard, as might be expected, approved of the annexation, and in his autobiography, he justified it on the grounds of incompetent Boer rule: 'As they could not govern themselves and were about to plunge South Africa into a bloody war, our intervention was necessary' (1926a, I, p. 96). The annexation took place on 12 April 1877, and on annexation day Haggard himself ran up the British flag.

About this same time Haggard began to make some decisions about his future. He seems to have felt a desire to remain an imperial administrator, and he was already beginning to taste the fruits of promotion, something that fuelled his ambition yet further. In June 1877 Haggard wrote to his father, telling him about his recent appointment as English Clerk to the Colonial Secretary's Office: 'My aim is of course to rise to the position of a Colonial Governor' (1926a, I. p. 102). At the age of twenty-one he was appointed Master and Registrar of the High Court of the Transvaal and again wrote to his father: 'I believe I am by far the youngest head of Department in South Africa' (1926a, I, p. 114). This job allowed him to travel through the countryside meeting Boer farmers and their families. Unfortunately, however, these visits to the Boers only reinforced Haggard's already biased views, as can be seen in his article 'A Visit to the Chief Secocoeni' (1887), which demeaned the Boers in no uncertain terms. These and other undiplomatic remarks, for which Haggard was criticized by Sir Bartle Frere, then High Commissioner and Governor of the Cape, made their way back to South Africa from Britain and did little to aid Boer–British relations.

In the meantime, the annexation had not only intensified antagonism between the Boers and the British, but it had also led to an armed clash between black and white. Once Shepstone had annexed the Transvaal, he took the Boer side against the Zulus in a Transvaal border dispute. Cetshwayo and his Zulu warriors gathered their forces along the border of the Transvaal for a battle with the white intruders. Bartle Frere was determined to crush the Zulu military force and demanded that the Zulus disband their army. When they refused, the British invaded Zululand. Disaster followed, for a battalion of British regulars (including units made up of blacks) was totally annihilated by

Zulus at the battle of Isandhlwana. Soon after, Haggard joined the Pretoria Horse, a mounted corps formed initially to patrol the Zulu border but instructed, ironically, to stay in Pretoria and defend it from a threatened rebellion by the Boers. Haggard claims, in *Cetywayo and His White Neighbours*, that the news of the British defeat at Isand-hlwana was received by the Boers 'with great and unconcealed rejoicing' (1896, p. 193). They had learned that the British were not invincible, and they were determined to do away with their foreign rulers. But in the end the anticipated rebellion did not materialize and the Pretoria Horse disbanded.

Before the Zulus were finally crushed and Cetshwayo captured in August 1879, Haggard decided to leave the service of the British Government in South Africa. The reasons for his decision are not entirely clear, although a failed love affair combined with the removal of Shepstone from office most certainly played a part. One year after returning to England, Haggard married Louisa Margitson and made some attempt to recover his post as Master of the High Court of the Transvaal; but Sir Garnet Wolseley, then Commissioner for South-East Africa with complete control over Natal and the Transvaal, turned him down. None the less, Haggard, his wife, servants, furniture, and a dog left England for South Africa in 1880. Haggard's intention was to farm ostriches, but he and his household arrived just in time to receive news of the Bronker's Spruit Boer ambush of some British reinforcement troops coming from Lydenburg. As Haggard says, 'the Transvaal was in open rebellion' (1926a, I, p. 175). They travelled up country to their house in Newcastle where they thought they would be safe, but they soon abandoned any hope of being out of danger. The British had been defeated at the Ingogo River, and the Boers were descending into Natal to attack the reinforcements. A group of 500 Boers took the farmhouse next to the Haggards. 'Night by night', he writes, 'sometimes in our clothes, we slept with about six horses saddled in the stable, loaded rifles leaning against the beds and revolvers beneath our pillows' (1926a, I, p. 185).

The battle of Majuba Hill in 1881, led by Major General Sir George Pomeroy-Colley, was the turning point in the rebellion. The British had already suffered two defeats, at Lang's Nek and at the Ingogo River, and general opinion, including Haggard's own, was that Colley was too eager to go into battle and did so before he was properly prepared. The military disaster at Majuba, says Haggard, might have been avoided: 'Had he [Colley] been content to wait, it was said at the time – and I for one believe – that the Boers would have melted away' (1926a, I, p. 186). This defeat, in his view, 'brought about the Retrocession' (1926a, I, p. 187). The subsequent negotiations lasted roughly five weeks and took place, oddly enough, at Hilldrop, Haggard's Newcastle home. Reflecting on the irony of the situation, Haggard remarked: 'It was a strange fate which decreed that the Retrocession of the Transvaal, over which I had myself hoisted the British flag, should be practically accomplished beneath my roof' (1926a, I, p. 190).

Back in England the following year, Haggard wrote his own account of the events surrounding the annexation and the retrocession, *Cetywayo and His White Neighbours*. His analysis of the inconclusive peace reached during the retrocession, combined with his criticism of the way Wolseley was administering Zululand, led him to predict that, unless the South African questions were 'treated with more honest intelligence . . . the British taxpayer will find that he has *by no means* heard the last of that country and its wars' (1896, p. lxxvii).

The retrocession was for Haggard what Gordon's death at Khartoum was to the British a few years later – a sign of Gladstone's treachery. What he saw around him at this time affected his notion of government and Empire thereafter. He describes the scene at the market square in Newcastle when people realized that the Transvaal was about to be returned to Boer rule: 'Some thousands of people were gathered there, many of them refugees, among them were a number of loyal Boers, and with these soldiers, townsfolk, and natives. I saw strong men weeping like children, and English-born people crying aloud that they were "b____y Englishmen" no more' (1926a, I, p. 194). Many people, Haggard recalled, clearly felt that they had been betrayed:

They could not believe their ears, in which still echoed the vehement declaration of Sir Garnet Wolseley that no Government would dare under any circumstances to give back the Transvaal, and other statements, in the House of Lords, by telegram, and in other ways of various members of the Administration to the same effect. (1926a, I, p. 194)

The retrocession was interpreted as desertion of the colonials by the imperial government. In Newcastle, by his own account, Haggard 'suffered the highest sort of shame, shame for my country' (1926a, I, p. 195).

Like his earlier plan to become a Colonial Governor, Haggard's somewhat more modest intention to become an ostrich farmer was thus altered. His return to England, as he explained in a letter of 30 July 1881 to his father, was due to 'the state of the country' (1926a, I, p. 201). Not only was he concerned with the precarious position he would be in if he were to stay, but he was deeply troubled by the feeling of disgrace he had experienced.

The path from imperial administrator and ostrich farmer to author was by no means direct. Once back in England, Haggard decided to read for the Bar. With the law experience he had had in the Transvaal, the decision made sense. Before long he also decided to set the South African record straight, according to his own lights. *Cetywayo*, Haggard's first book (he agreed to pay fifty pounds towards its publication), prompted the following expression of thanks from Lord Carnarvon:

The English public was so deceived by misrepresentations of the annexation of the Transvaal that the real history was never understood; and the humiliating surrender of it was accepted in partial ignorance at least of the facts ... I am grateful to anyone who has the courage to say what really did occur. (12 May 1888, Columbia Collection)

Haggard tried his hand at fiction next, but the reviews of *Dawn*, a story of country life, were not encouraging. He had yet to discover that his talents were in the field of adventure writing. He had better luck – and better reviews – with his second effort at fiction, *The Witch's Head*, part of which is set in South Africa during the Zulu War. Reviewers pointed to the African sections as showing signs of promise in this new writer.[2] Shortly afterwards, however, he passed his Bar examinations and thought seriously about giving up fiction altogether in favour of his new profession.

At about the same time that he passed the Bar, Haggard read a notice of *Treasure Island* that drew his attention to this much-admired book and led him to try a boys' adventure of his own, *King Solomon's Mines*. Doubtless his financial situation had something to do with these new plans. He was evidently convinced, by this time, of the severity of the agricultural crisis. 'The bad years were upon us', he explained in *The Days of My Life*, 'and rents fell rapidly' (1926a, I,

p. 220). But if Haggard, now the father of three, was motivated by financial security, he was also impelled by an unmistakable penchant for the writing of fiction itself. Once completed, the manuscript of *King Solomon's Mines* reached William Ernest Henley, then editor of Cassell's *Magazine of Art*. Eventually it was published by Cassell's and this time the reviews were overwhelmingly positive. Andrew Lang's notice in the *Saturday Review* was unreservedly enthusiastic: 'We have only praise for the very remarkable and uncommon powers of invention and gift of "vision" which Mr. Haggard displays' (10 October 1885, p. 485). An anonymous reviewer in the *Athenaeum* found in it 'some fighting hardly to be beaten outside Homer and the great Dumas' and declared that 'we should be surprised if it does not also prove to be the best [book of the season]' (31 October 1885, p. 568). A more sober opinion came to Haggard in a letter from Robert Louis Stevenson, who was, coincidentally, a friend of Haggard's brother Bazett in Samoa. Along with offering praise for the book's 'flashes of fine weird imagination and a fine poetic use and command of the savage way of talking', he urged Haggard to 'be more careful; you do quite well enough to take more trouble' (1926a, I, p. 235).

Unfortunately, however, Haggard disregarded Stevenson's good advice. He wrote most of his fiction at a reckless speed with about as much concern for language as a whirlwind for the victims left in its wake. *Allan Quatermain* was written during a summer holiday in 1885. As for *She*, Haggard tells us, 'the whole romance was written at white heat, almost without rest, and that is the best way to compose' (1926a, I, p. 245). With his usual lack of anything resembling modesty, he sums up his prodigious activities of a year and a half:

It would seem, therefore, that between January 1885 and March 18, 1886, with my own hand, and unassisted by any secretary, I wrote 'King Solomon's Mines', 'Allan Quatermain', 'Jess', and 'She'. Also I followed my profession, spending many hours of each day studying in chambers, or in court, where I had some devilling practice, carried on my usual correspondence, and attended to the affairs of a man with a young family and a certain landed estate.   (1926a, I, p. 246)

By 1886, Haggard's success was assured, allowing him to write thereafter with the confidence that dependable remuneration is apt to inspire. And money was certainly of primary concern. Unlike writers who secure jobs to support their writing, Haggard wrote to support his other interests. The romances sold well, and Haggard soon earned enough money by writing to leave his law office and devote his time to gardening, farming, and agricultural research. He more than satisfied his passion for travel, often gathering information or merely saturating himself in the atmosphere as a prelude to some piece of fiction. His trip to Egypt in 1887 resulted in *Cleopatra* (1889), and his voyage to Iceland in 1888 was followed by his saga *Eric Brighteyes* (1891). His journey to Mexico in 1890 provided him with the material for *Montezuma's Daughter* (1893), and his tour of Florence, Cyprus, and Palestine in 1900 resulted in *Pearl Maiden* (1903) and *The Brethren* (1904). *A Winter Pilgrimage* (1901), a travel book, was also written from notes made during this trip. Haggard returned to Egypt in 1904 and wandered up the Nile visiting temples and tombs. This journey led to *The Way of the Spirit* (1906) and *Morning Star* (1910). He returned home via Italy and Spain, and *Fair Margaret* (1907), with its Spanish setting, was the result.

Politics first beckoned Haggard in 1893 when he was asked to contest the seat of King's Lynn. He declined because the expense of going to and from the borough was felt to be too costly, but he agreed to stand for Parliament in 1895, this time for East Norfolk, a constituency he described as 'one of the most difficult in the kingdom from the Conservative point of view' (1926a, II, p. 111). He lost (by 198 votes) on a programme that was Unionist and agricultural. The campaign experience disagreed with Haggard and destroyed any interest he had in public office. He was especially disgusted by what he called the 'indirect corruption' (1926a, II, p. 115) involved in the business of selling a candidate and concluded that he was not a 'party' man. His work for Empire would have to be done on the periphery of party circles. He also believed that certain contradictions in his views would render him unacceptable to any party. He had strong feelings for the labouring poor, but he detested Radicalism. He was in general agreement with Tory principles, but he favoured a scheme of small land holdings which meant the destruction of many estates. Such views, he thought, were not in keeping with party politics.

Throughout his life, Haggard's name was associated with South Africa. His fiction and *Cetywayo and His White Neighbours*, in conjunction with certain speeches and letters to various newpapers, established this link. He became co-director of the *African Review*, a weekly paper, and it was understood by his fellow-director that, had he won the East Norfolk seat, he would have given his attention to African affairs. Haggard was also elected to chair the Anglo-African Writers' Club, and during the Boer War, *The Times* asked him to be a war correspondent, although he declined because of his age. He subsequently arranged with Arthur Pearson, owner of the *Daily Express*, to do a series on 'The New South Africa' at the conclusion of the War. But the fighting was slow to end, and Pearson suggested a cancellation of the contract. When Haggard responded with a proposal to substitute a series of articles on rural England, Pearson agreed. In this way, Haggard came to write *Rural England*, for which he journeyed from farm to farm for months on end, investigating the state of the countryside. The series ran in the *Daily Express* as promised, making his name as a committed agricultural reformer.

Haggard was often able to combine his love of travel with his work as a public servant. He went to the United States in 1905 when he was made Commissioner to the U.S.A. to inspect and report on labour colonies founded by the Salvation Army in Colorado, Ohio, and California. During this trip Haggard met and established his friendship with the then President, Theodore Roosevelt, who was interested in South African politics, according to Haggard, because of his Dutch descent. Roosevelt expressed his liking for *Rural England* at this time, and in later years often wrote Haggard to praise one of his new books. When Haggard returned to England with a colonization scheme, Balfour's government refused funds for Salvation Army work and scrapped his recommendations. This rejection added to Haggard's abiding scepticism of government: 'I never even received a letter of thanks', he recalled afterwards, and in the end 'all came to nothing' (1926a, II, pp. 197, 203).

In 1906 he was appointed to another Royal Commission, initially to study coastal erosion, although one year later the question of afforestation was added to the Commission's frame of reference. To Haggard's disappointment, the afforestation scheme of the Commission, produced in advance of its work on coastal erosion, was not adopted by the government, and the coastal erosion project continued for five more years. (Like the proposals on afforestation, the final recommendations of the Royal Commission on Coastal Erosion were shelved.) In the meantime, Haggard began another project for the Salvation Army, a report on their institutional work later published as *Regeneration* (1910), and he undertook yet another agricultural study, *Rural Denmark* (1911), a book commending Danish policies on small holdings and credit banks.

Haggard's name appeared in the New Year's Honours List of 1912, which he considered just recognition for his years of service. In the same year he was asked to be a member of a Royal Commission to tour the Empire, studying trade and agriculture. This, he records, was 'recognition – with a vengeance' (1926a, II, p. 227). Ironically, this appointment was made by a Radical government. Haggard travelled as a Commissioner for some years, visiting India, Canada, Newfoundland, Australia, New Zealand, and Africa. When the Commission toured South Africa in 1914, Haggard was accompanied by his wife, Louie, and youngest daughter, Lilias, and he spent much of his time visiting remembered sights and calling on old friends. For Haggard, who was inclined to be nostalgic, this was an especially moving experience. The last of his official work for Empire occurred in 1916 when the Royal Colonial Institute sent him to South Africa, Australia, New Zealand, and Canada to see about settling ex-servicemen in the Dominions after the war.

All of this, as Haggard himself might say, was accomplished while he was writing one, two, or even three romances a year. (When he died he had four manuscripts ready for publication.) Clearly, Haggard's capacity for strenuous living was almost inexhaustible. He was not the sort of man who could easily put aside his gardening and farming, agricultural projects, touring, government work, and family responsibilities to devote himself wholly to the job of writing fiction. In January 1924 he made one last trip to Egypt, returning home in April to attend the business of public addresses at luncheons and dinners. It was after one of these luncheons, the bicentenary celebration for Longmans, Green & Co. in November 1924, that Haggard fell ill. He died six months later on 14 May 1925, reducing the diminishing ranks of old imperialists by one.

THE IMPERIAL BACKGROUND

The age of British imperialism, the historical backdrop against which I will set Haggard's romances, extends from about 1870 to 1914. Bounding one end of the period is the Franco-Prussian War, the conclusion of which, in 1873, gave French and German manufacturing interests the opportunity to launch an attack on Britain's commercial monopoly. In this way a new era of national – soon to be imperial – rivalry among nations was inaugurated. During the decades immediately before 1914, the imposition of foreign rule on subject peoples went on apace; never before was an age quite so indifferent to the claims of territorial integrity.

Although there were assorted internal pressures that drove Great Britain into an identifiably new era after 1870, the external pressures exerted by the Franco-Prussian War were probably the most critical. The historian R. C. K. Ensor tells us that 'When the guns of the Franco-Prussian War first thundered on 4 August 1870 a new epoch began' (1936, p. ix). This new epoch distinguished itself by certain military, economic, and political changes. In military terms, Ensor says, the war 'gave the world a new conception of war's possibilities as an instrument of policy under modern, highly organized conditions' (1936, p. ix). The war was partially responsible for the reorganization of the British army and, in much of the rest of Europe, led to the adoption of military conscription. Its effect was to introduce a new military mentality.

This military challenge to British security was multiplied many times over by the economic shock of the post-war era. Monopoly control of the market, on which so much of Britain's free-trading policies depended, could not continue indefinitely. Britain's expanded productive forces had to contend with the re-entry of France and Germany into the commercial market. The United States, having recovered from its own Civil War, was an additional factor in commercial competition. Moreover, France, Germany, and the United States soon erected tariff walls. Thus, while free trade worked to Britain's advantage under conditions of monopoly, it proved less advantageous in a highly competitive atmosphere. Agriculture suffered even more than industry, a factor which concerned Haggard, whose own feelings about this period were shaped by his agrarian interests. There were occasional booms at the end of the 1880s and the 1890s, but not for agriculture. Periodic economic crises dampened what remained of mid-Victorian optimism, and such confidence could never again be revived.

As with the military consequences of the Franco-Prussian War, the economic consequences helped to intensify national rivalry. The cosmopolitan outlook that was associated with *laissez-faire* Liberalism fell out of favour when free trade failed to reward such supra-national generosity. A gradual conversion to nationalism was made by those who felt increasingly uneasy about the future of free markets. The seeds of a protectionist movement were sown. National rivalry was aggravated still further following the Franco-Prussian War by the freedom given to France and Germany to compete with Britain for foreign territory. Thus, military, economic, and national expansion was intensified seemingly of necessity.

Haggard, from his position as landowner and farmer, viewed the domestic situation pre-eminently as an agricultural crisis. His class, which had been at odds with the Liberals since the repeal of the Corn Laws, had done little about the protection issue since then because, despite predictions to the contrary, agriculture had prospered during the decades that followed repeal. Haggard was among those for whom the depression in agriculture revived the free trade debate. In *Rural England*, he said that the ruination of agriculture was caused by 'unchecked foreign competition' (1902, II, p. 536). Although countries like France and Germany had put up trade barriers for imports from the United States, South America, New Zealand, and Russia, Britain had not. 'Remember', wrote Haggard, 'that the foreigner has but one market for his superfluous stores – the British Isles' (1902, II, p. 537). As for free trade, Haggard observed, 'Whatever Free Trade may have done for the country at large – and I maintain that of this matter we do not as yet know all the truth – it is certain that it has brought the land and the agriculture of England very near to the brink of ruin' (1902, II, p. 564). The opposition between landowner and manufacturer or, as in the following passage, between rural and urban sectors, very naturally followed from the general attack on free trade. 'Free Trade', Haggard continued, 'has filled the towns and emptied the countryside; it has gorged the Banks but left our rick-yards bare' (1902, II, p. 564).

Still another problem for Haggard, hinted at in his remarks on free trade, was the migration of rural labourers to the cities, an issue he linked to ideas of nation, militarism, and race. Haggard perceived the rural exodus as marking the ruin of both the English race and nation: 'But behind the agricultural question lies the national question. What will be the result of this desertion of the countryside and of the crowding of its denizens into the cities? . . . It can mean nothing less than the progressive deterioration of the race' (1902, II, p. 541). Moreover, physical deterioration meant, above all else, a threat to national security. He pointedly illustrated the ill effects of urban living by comparing the hardy country-bred men with the less fit town-reared men reporting for service in the Boer War at the London recruiting office. Urban men were at a similar disadvantage when they encountered the rural Boers. Haggard was 'convinced . . . that most of our reverses during the recent [Boer] war were due to the pitting of town-bred bodies and intelligences, both of officers and men, against the country-bred bodies and intelligences' (1902, II, p. 568). He was also convinced that unless the British changed, the Dutch would eventually control South Africa precisely because they were people of the soil. The nature of Haggard's attitude towards rural life is apparent, finally, when viewed in the context of his belief that the rural or 'natural condition is better than the artificial [that is, urban] condition' (1902, II, p. 564). The material prosperity achieved in the urban and industrial regions of England could not compare, for him, with the human resources of the countryside, especially as a factor in promoting national well-being: 'after all', he wrote, 'men and women sound in body and equal if slow in mind, are of more importance to a country than any material wealth' (1902, II, p. 564).

The threat of 'foreigners' and the fear of a degenerating race are by no means isolated features of Haggard's picture of agricultural depression. They can be made to stand alongside others in a much larger portrait of the period to demonstrate the strong affinity of ideas which form the imperialist mentality. Indeed, the nation's military security is seen to be dependent on the state of agriculture. After constant pleading for his cause, replete with warnings of racial and every other kind of degeneration, Haggard revealed the ultimate weapon of his agricultural crusade – the threat of a European war. England's dependency on foreign produce would be disastrous during wartime: 'I am convinced', he wrote, 'that the risk of starvation which might strike our Country in the event of a European War, is no mere spectre of the alarmist' (1902, II, p. 560).[3] This last remark appears to have been made with some foresight given the German submarine campaign of the First World War, but prescience aside, advancing agriculture in the guise of military necessity, which Haggard had been doing from the early 1890s onwards, was a questionable expedient.

The meshing of ideas and attitudes in Haggard reflects in miniature

19

the conjunction of ideas and attitudes of the imperial age. Although it is impossible to present a tidy picture of imperialism and its mirror image in Haggard's writings, some awareness of how imperialism drew together the sundry elements of class conflict, domestic policy, party politics, and all manner of socio-economic phenomena within the sphere of foreign policy is crucial to the understanding of Haggard's fiction in the imperial context. Indeed, this unifying quality of imperialism is its own governing feature.

The significance of class warfare in determining the character of late nineteenth-century imperialism cannot be overlooked. The threat of class war was strongly felt and was in part, no doubt, another by-product of the Franco-Prussian War, at the end of which the workers of the Paris Commune tried to hold the city against the French state. Imperialists realized that something had to be done to improve class relations and, more specifically, to turn the working class away from socialism and its divisive doctrine of class conflict. Instead of risking the destruction of their power, they agreed to certain reforms. It was vital to convince workers that their interests lay in supporting the Empire and transferring their allegiance from class to nation. Cecil Rhodes's remarks in a speech made to the Charter Company in 1892 aimed at this: 'The idea that the taking up of the uncivilized portions of the world is to the advantage of the classes is erroneous; the proceeding is entirely to the advantage of the masses' ('Imperialist', 1897, p. 369). And in the same speech: 'I desire to point out to you that it is your duty, wherever and whenever you can, to impress upon the masses that this question of keeping control of the outer world is a matter of pleasure to the classes, but that it is a question of life to the masses' ('Imperialist', 1897, p. 372).

Rhodes's brand of imperialism, expressed candidly if crudely, is merely a less polished version of other more successfully articulated attempts at class collaboration. Milner, for example, more rhetorically adroit than Rhodes, publicly denounced class warfare and couched his criticism in the language of social reform. In a speech delivered to the Manchester Conservative Club in December 1906, he said:

Yes. By all means social reform. But where is the antagonism between it and imperialism? To my mind they are inseparable ideals, and absolutely inter-dependent and complementary to one another. How are you going to sustain this vast fabric of the Empire? No single class can sustain it. It needs the strength of the whole people. (Milner, 1913, p. 139)

In another speech, also delivered in December 1906, Milner discussed his idea of a 'nobler Socialism':

That there is an odious form of Socialism I admit, a Socialism which attacks wealth simply because it is wealth, and lives on the cultivation of class hatred. But that is not the whole story, most assuredly not. There is a nobler Socialism, which so far from springing from 'envy, hatred, and all uncharitableness', is born of genuine sympathy and a lofty and wise conception of what is meant by national life. It realizes the fact that we are not merely so many millions of individuals, each struggling for himself, with the State to act as Policeman, but literally one body-politic; that the different classes and sections of the community are members of that body, and that when one member suffers all the members suffer.   (1913, p. 161)

Finally, in 1912, Milner addressed an audience at Toynbee Hall, a social settlement in East London, reiterating the same theme:

I am not one of those who think that what is known as the solidarity of the workers of all nations, the substitution of class divisions for national or racial divisions, is going to ensure national peace or to promote the happiness of mankind. I believe in development along national lines, and I believe in the mission of my country, of the British race – that it stands for something distinctive and priceless in the outward march of humanity. My chief reason for detesting any form of social cleavage, I don't say it is my only reason, is that it weakens my country.   (1913, p. 496)

It bears repeating that the movement towards and achievement of unity is the outstanding characteristic of imperialism. The unity of the state helps to solidify its power, justify its practices, and mythologize its greatness. It is the requisite factor for the nationalism that transforms itself into imperialism, the patriotism that becomes jingoism. The consolidated national state, with its emphasis on racial unity, succeeded in fostering British exclusiveness both at home and abroad. The racial bond was the glue to bind the states of Empire together. Like the plea to place nation above class, the argument for racial unity had the sound of good imperial salesmanship. Why encourage national integrity in the states of Empire and create future administrative problems when encouraging racial unity paves the way for self-imposed control emanating from the states themselves and maintains the central British authority? This, of course, is what the race issue comes to in terms of practical politics. Many English people, however, probably believed their ideas of racial unity to be perfectly humane. C. W. Dilke, for example, in his *Greater Britain*, 'followed England round the world', and was warmed to find that in America, Australia, India, and Canada, 'in essentials the race was always one' (1869, p. v). However irreproachable their subjective feelings may have been, later critics have judged them on more objective grounds.

Milner, whose ideal was for the states of Empire to be 'in a permanent organic union' (1913, p. 91), held forth on the race issue with predictable references to blood and tradition: 'Not that I underestimate the importance of community of material interests in binding the different parts of the Empire together. . . . But deeper, stronger, and more primordial than these material ties is the bond of common blood, a common language, common history and traditions' (1913, p. xxxv). If the virulence of race propaganda originally escaped notice when it applied primarily to white nations, it was plainly apparent when white came into contact with black in Africa. Even in 1916, however, Haggard was arguing in the same vein as Milner. He proposed during the First World War that ex-servicemen be resettled as farmers in the overseas dominions, another means, he claimed, by which to relieve the agricultural situation. During his travels to the Cape, according to his report on the overseas resettlement plan, he found 'a general desire for more white population in their Union' (1916, p. 4). (He specifically stated that white *working-men* ought not to emigrate inasmuch as their doing the same work as black men would push the value of white work down and that of black work up.) Offers from the dominions to resettle white men on their land were seen as examples 'to the world of that unity of aim and spirit which now . . . pervades the British Empire' (1916, p. 39). Clearly the aim and spirit of Empire were united, at least in part, by a racist ideology.

Still another facet of this phenomenon of consolidation which belongs to the idea of the imperial state is the union between the state and the economy. Rhodes, for example, as managing director of the British South Africa Company, wanted the rights to more land in southern Africa, for which he needed sanction from London. In return for this official approval, historians Ronald Robinson and John Gallagher tell us in *Africa and the Victorians*, 'he offered to finance, administer and colonise Matabeleland on behalf of the Cape

Colony, to take over the Bechuanaland Protectorate from the Colonial Office and to extend the Bechuanaland railway and telegraph to the Zambesi River' (1961, p. 237). Eventually, the British South Africa Company Charter of 1889–91 gave him 'full financial and administrative responsibility for the countries . . . "lying immediately to the north of British Bechuanaland . . . to the north and west of the South African Republic and to the west of the Portuguese Dominions"' (1961, p. 243). The subordination of all else to the exigencies of Empire was taken into account by C. F. G. Masterman, who, in one of a selection of essays on imperialism in *The Heart of the Empire* (1901), looked back on the eighties, when the franchise and trade union bills were passed, as years of promise that were never fulfilled and years of Empire in the making:

One who had gone to sleep in the middle of that stirring time and suddenly awakened at the commencement of the twentieth century might be pardoned if on rubbing his eyes and gazing on the present ideals and conditions of society he maintained that he was still dreaming. For a wave of 'Imperialism' has swept the country, and all these efforts, hopes, and visions have vanished as if wiped out with a sponge. (1901, p. 3)

The most progressive ideas were mere appendages on the body of Empire. Herbert Branston Gray, for instance, in a 1913 book on educational reform, *The Public Schools and the Empire*, recommended changing the scholarship funds and the competitive system as well as eliminating the cult of sport. Gray was also strongly in favour of an educational programme which would provide students with a foundation in the sciences and economics. Curiously, all of his arguments for reform were advanced in the name of Empire, for the integrity of Empire, and for the education of the best rulers of Empire.

The state of the parliamentary system during the imperial period also illustrates the movement to unite and solidify. Power drifted towards and concentrated at the centre, a result of the specialized nature of imperial affairs which narrowed the circle of informed decision makers. Party colleagues left behind carried on an opposition more apparent than real. In Hannah Arendt's view, imperialism 'was the chief cause of the degeneration of the two-party system into the Front Bench system' (1958, p. 153). Dissension in the Liberal Party, a clear sign of this degeneration, assumed unmistakable crisis proportions in 1886 during the Home Rule controversy. Subsequent to the defeat of Gladstone's Home Rule bill, Chamberlain and others, plainly antagonistic to the 'little Englander' attitude of the Gladstonian bloc, resigned and formed the Unionist Party. (However much Gladstone may be accused by Haggard of playing havoc with the stability of Empire, the Liberal interludes under his leadership did not see any wholesale renunciation of territory.) With Chamberlain gone and Gladstone retired, the schism in the Liberal ranks was promoted by Lord Rosebery and Campbell-Bannerman, Rosebery leading the maverick Liberal Imperialist faction which endorsed an expansionist but free trade policy.

Some imperialists felt they were beyond party. In 1905, Rosebery enunciated his critique of the political party in the foreword to Alfred Stead's *Great Japan*: 'I do not seek to abolish party. I recognize it as part of our moral climate; but we must ever bear in mind that when we aim at efficiency we shall be handicapped by this formidable encumbrance' (Raymond, 1923, pp. 209–10). Like classes, parties could cause a rent to appear in the imperial fabric, create division and disunity. Milner was not a defender of the party system either. A man who viewed the squabbles of parties from disinterested heights, Milner believed that 'party politics were a meaningless struggle between the ins and outs, a struggle having little to do with principles' (Crankshaw, 1952, pp. 135–6). He is also credited with having remarked that 'the influence of representative assemblies, organized upon the party system, upon administration – "government" in the true sense of the word – is uniformly bad' (LeMay, 1965, p. 10). As will be clear in the following chapter, Haggard was another one of those who were partial to the idea of supra-party politics.

Two books on imperialism of exceptional note and of especial relevance to this discussion are Elie Halévy's *Imperialism and the Rise of Labour* (1926) and Hannah Arendt's *The Origins of Totalitarianism* (1958). Aside from the fresh insights which Halévy brings to bear on familiar material, the outstanding contribution he makes in this book is what he considers to be a new concept of the state. He roots this new concept in the rising idealism and turning from positivism of the age, as expressed by people like Bernard Bosanquet in his *The Philosophical Theory of the State* (1899) and Benjamin Kidd in his neo-Darwinist writings. Popular defences of this idealism, Halévy argues, can be found in the works of Robert Louis Stevenson, W. E. Henley, and Rudyard Kipling. (He makes no mention of Haggard, their personal friend and fellow imperialist.) He calls these men the 'authentic interpreters of the prevalent attitude' (1926, p. 20), and cites Kipling's *Jungle Books* in particular as 'a species of Darwinian philosophy expressed in mythical form [which created] the foundation of a moral code, chaste, brutal, heroic, and childlike' (1926, p. 21). The thrust of this idealism is not simply the undermining of materialist interpretations of reality but the erection of a monumental image of the state as an object of reverence wholly idealized and above the petty problems of every day.

What causes Hannah Arendt's study to be so markedly different from Halévy's is its historical proximity to the present age. Having come through the Second World War, she turns to the earlier era of imperialism as a potential source of twentieth-century totalitarianism. She charges the nineteenth century with developing, along with its nationalism, the kind of 'race thinking' now associated with Nazi Germany. 'Race thinking', a term to be distinguished from racism, is a kind of national sectarianism associated with the colonization of Australia, New Zealand, and Canada. Racism, on the other hand, she suggests, came into being when white people colonized black territories and needed to develop a system of control. Fully aware of the inadequacies of a 'racial' interpretation of imperialism, Hannah Arendt none the less develops arguments linking racism and imperialism which are altogether convincing, especially those regarding the South African situation.

The idealism identified by Halévy is discernible yet again in the area of racism. According to Hannah Arendt, the idea of 'the white man's burden', for example, inspired the loyalty of many imperialists for whom the Empire conferred a spiritual reward as much as a material one. Such was the case with Milner, who claimed that England's position as a leader of Empire was

of inestimable value . . . less perhaps for the material benefits which it brings us than for its effect upon the national character – for it has helped to develop some of the best, most distinctive qualities of the race . . . Our share of "the white man's burden" is an exceptional share. No doubt it is good for us to bear it. (Milner, 1913, p. xxxiii)

The British even prided themselves on a kind of racial fairness, although it saw plenty of service as a mask for self-interest, as is apparent in Jameson's naive or hypocritical estimation of Rhodes as 'deeply in sympathy with the natives. He regards them as children with something of pity in his affection for them and he treats them like children, affectionately but firmly' ('Imperialist', 1897, p. 404).

The concealing of economic and political concerns behind a rhetorical cover of either national or racial superiority is hardly peculiar to the British Empire, but it did coincide, as we have seen in Halévy, with a resurgence of philosophical idealism. Heinz Gollwitzer also writes of Oxford 'neo-idealism', as exemplified by men such as T. H. Green, Herbert Bradley, and Bernard Bosanquet, in his *The Age of Imperialism, 1880–1914*:

The main theme of this school of thought may be identified as the historical determinism of the universe, and not least of the state and justice; the concept of the historical–social universe as an organism; the primacy of man's ethical nature, his strength of will and his moral motivation; the existence of a metaphysical unity. The historical–philosophic constructions of this school give the conception of Empire – primarily the British Empire of course – an elevated status, indeed the highest place among all manifestations of social organization. (1969, pp. 154–5)

In other words, idealism posits a metaphysical conception of causality, and the Empire, an expression of supersensible, co-ordinated and motive power, is understood to be working out the design of some transcendental force.

Gollwitzer names Milner as one of the 'Oxford students stamped with the spirit of Neo-idealism' (1969, p. 155). Such idealism is not difficult to illustrate. Milner, for whom imperialism was a 'creed' (1913, p. 138), revealed his messianic conception of Empire in the introduction to *The Nation and the Empire* (1913), a collection of his speeches:

Imperialism as a political doctrine has often been represented as something tawdry and superficial. In reality it has all the depth and comprehensiveness of a religious faith. Its significance is moral even more than material. It is a mistake to think of it as principally concerned with extension of territory, with "painting the map red". There is quite enough painted red already. It is not a question of a couple of hundred square miles more or less. It is a question of preserving the unity of a great race, of enabling it, by maintaining that unity, to develop freely on its own lines, and continue to fulfil its distinctive mission in the world. (1913, p. xxxii)

The most famous example of this imperial idealism is found in Lord Rosebery's speech to the students of the University of Glasgow in 1900:

How marvellous it all is! Built not by saints and angels, but the work of men's hands; cemented with men's honest blood and with a world of tears, welded by the best brains of centuries past; not without taint and reproach incidental to all human work, but constructed on the whole with pure and splendid purpose. Human and yet not wholly human, for the most heedless and the most cynical must see the finger of the divine. Growing as trees while others slept; fed by the faults of others as well as by the character of our own fathers; and reaching with the ripple of a resistless tide over tracts and islands and continents until our little Britain woke up to find herself the foster mother of nations and the source of limited empires. Do we not hail in this less the energy and fortune of a race than the supreme direction of the Almighty? Shall we not, while we adore the blessing, acknowledge the responsibility? And while we see, far away in the rich horizons, growing generations fulfilling the promise, do we not own with resolution mingled with awe the honourable duty incumbent on ourselves? Shall we then falter and fail? The answer is not doubtful. We will rather pray that strength be given us, adequate and abundant, to shrink from no sacrifice in the fulfilment of our mission that we may transmit their bequest to our children, ay, and please God, to their remote descendants enriched and undefiled, this blessed and splendid dominion.   (Raymond, 1923, p. 71)

There is no imperial book-keeping here, no accounts kept, no incidental discussion of trade or even strategy. All is lost in the rhetoric of self-denial, obedience, and responsibility.

Idealism was not out of keeping with economic interests. What the age needed was a mid-Victorian ethic of trade altered to something more amenable to the spirit. Imperialism had to be good business, but it had to be good for the soul as well. It had to be more elevating than mid-century commercialism while yielding the same material benefits. Idealism, then, was well suited to the purposes of the age, though on its own, perhaps, a dangerous philosophical movement. Consider the comments of L. T. Hobhouse, one of the most persuasive anti-imperialists, in his *Democracy and Reaction* (1904):

in the main, the idealistic movement has swelled the currents of retrogression. It is itself, in fact, one expression of the general reaction against the plain, human, rationalistic way of looking at life and its problems. Every institution and every belief is for it alike a manifestation of a spiritual principle, and thus for everything there is an inner and more spiritual interpretation. Hence, vulgar and stupid beliefs can be held with a refined and enlightened meaning, known only to him who so holds them.   (p. 78)

Hobhouse's statement hits upon the bullying aspect of idealism: you either understand and believe something to be so, or you do not – there is no demand for ideas to be upheld by demonstrable fact or logical discourse. By and large, then, idealism contains the seeds of authoritarianism.

An extension of this variety of intellectual tyranny is the age's emphasis on leadership and heroism. Chamberlain could say that 'the Anglo-Saxon race is infallibly destined to be the predominant force in history and civilization of the world' (Hobson, 1965, p. 160). (The black person's destiny, says Hobhouse, 'is to assist in the development of gold mines for the benefit of humanity in general and the shareholders in particular' [1904, pp. 62–3].) Military men such as Gordon, Kitchener, Roberts, and Buller were hailed as great figures of the day. Set apart as it was from the commonplace world of bureaucratic decision making, soldiering could become an image of individual daring and strength, a symbol of the spiritual destiny of Empire. An age in need of heroes, it took these men for the instruments of a greater will. By 1907, boys who used to play at soldiering would join the more organized ranks of the Boy Scouts, a movement endorsed by Haggard and Kipling and cheered by H. G. Wells's imperialist Richard Remington in *The New Machiavelli* (1911). Battle itself becomes a purifying activity. Wells's Remington says of a European war: 'I pray for a chastening war – I wouldn't mind her [England's] flag in the dirt if only her spirit would come out of it' (Wells, 1946, p. 267). Haggard agrees, and in fact saw the First World War as vindicating his own views of battle. In his diary of 16 January 1915 he notes:

In some ways I think the war is doing good in England. It is bringing the people, or some of them, face to face with elementary facts which hitherto it has been the fashion to ignore and pretend are non-existent. To take one very humble example. How often have I been vituperated by rose-water critics because I have written of fighting and tried to inculcate certain elementary lessons, such as that it is a man's duty to defend his country and that only those who are prepared for war can protect themselves and such as are dear to them.   (Haggard Diaries, 16 January 1915)

We turn finally to consider the well-known and often-quoted statement of 1883 by Sir John Seeley, that the Empire was created 'in a fit of absence of mind' (1971, p. 12). The full statement, 'We seem, as it were, to have conquered and peopled half the world in a fit of absence of mind', is generally taken to mean that there was no coherent system or master plan devised early in the imperial age which dictated policy. In my attempt to show that imperialism grew from certain historical conditions of the period, I have implicitly rejected the view of history as something that conforms to a pre-conceived idea. However, I believe that a recognizable imperialist ideology was gradually developed, and that the ideas of Empire which evolved during the period gained enough currency to become settled as the typical beliefs of British society. The contributions of Rider Haggard aided this process to no small degree.

Chapter 2

THE POLITICS OF ROMANCE

Fictional romance prefers the past to the present, forgoes the prosaic for the wonderful, and appeals more to the senses than to the mind. In Haggard, romance favours the form of the adventure story, the particular attraction of which is its movement, its action, and its striking and colourful contrast with ordinary routine. Edward Shanks, who said in his 1927 essay on Haggard that the adventure story was newly invigorated during the late nineteenth century, claimed that Haggard helped 'the victims of modern civilization to find the adventure and variety and unexpectedness ... denied to them in ordinary life' (1927, p. 128). Romance is also, then, a means of escape.

For Haggard, the escapist nature of romance needed no justification; it was a given of the genre. His own reading public, he thought, was especially inclined towards such literary diversion. 'More and more', Haggard wrote, 'as what we call culture spreads, do man and woman crave to be taken out of themselves' (1887a, p. 174). And again, 'a weary public continually calls for books, new books to make them forget, to refresh them, to occupy minds jaded with ... toil and emptiness and vexation' (1887a, p. 174). By this 'weary public' Haggard seems to have meant people like himself, whose financial stability was faltering and who faced, perhaps for the first time, insecurity and fear, men like the fictional Sir Henry Curtis in *Allan Quatermain*, a squire in a country that increasingly had no use for squires.

To some extent, the escapist character of Haggard's romances can also be related to a personal sense of frustration with his society's growing attachment to machines, industry, and urban living. Haggard may be seen as the representative voice of a dying agricultural tradition, a role which prepares him to be the new voice of imperialism. His writing satisfied much the same need that was satisfied by the outpourings of Milner and Rosebery, the need for a fuller emotional existence in an increasingly oppressive and matter-of-fact industrial society. For those like Haggard, who faced the passing of a rural existence, the imperial landscape became more and more appealing. One could easily transfer one's sympathies to the non-industrial – hence more satisfying and enlivening – refuge of Empire.

Romance was excitement and wonder generated by newly discovered or still to be discovered regions of the world. Its emotional lure was unfailingly seductive. Africa especially seemed sufficiently far away to be strange; yet it was sufficiently real to hold out the promise of romance in life itself. The *Spectator* of 28 April 1888, for instance, recounting a story from *The Times* of an attack upon an English mission in Africa, described it as 'simply chapters iii. to viii. in "Allan Quatermain" rewritten' ('Reality and Romance', p. 570) and suggested that the tradition of an undiscovered white people such as the one in *Allan Quatermain* was 'apt to have a base of reality' (p. 571). In addition to the thrill of hazard that these foreign regions appeared to offer was the enticing freedom of an undeveloped landscape. Allan Quatermain, explaining his desire to leave England for Africa, makes the point:

no man who has for forty years lived the life I have can with impunity go coop himself in this prim English country, with its stiff formal manners, and its well-dressed crowds. He begins to long for the keen breath of the desert air; he dreams of the sight of Zulu impis breaking on their foes like surf upon the rocks, and his heart arises in rebellion against the strict limits of the civilised life.   (1919a, p. 12)

Like the soldier-speaker of Kipling's 'Mandalay', who seeks to be restored to 'a cleaner, greener land', Haggard's characters crave a world of excitement and sensuousness to replace the monotony and emptiness of their own.

Besides the emotional satisfaction associated with a reprieve from urban existence and the chance for a life of action, the Empire seemed to offer a source of wisdom. The romance of the 'noble savage' was rekindled; the simpler, more natural, 'uncivilized' quality of the non-western world made it seem closer, perhaps, to the essence of being that was hidden behind the spangles, draperies, and ornaments of English life. The 'savage', Allan Quatermain suggests in *Child of Storm* (1913), propounds a living lesson in the fundamentals of human nature:

We white people think that we know everything. For instance, we think that we understand human nature. And so we do, as human nature appears to us, with all its trappings and accessories seen dimly through the glass of our own conventions, leaving out those aspects of it we have forgotten or do not think it polite to mention. But I, Allan Quatermain . . . have always held that no one really understands human nature who has not studied it in the rough.

(Haggard, 1952, p. 1)

In the 'savage', he continues, 'nakedly and forcibly expressed, we see those eternal principles which direct our human destiny' (1952, p. 2). Since Haggard admitted in his autobiography that Quatermain was 'only myself set in a variety of imagined situations, thinking my thoughts and looking at life through my eyes' (1926a, II, pp. 85–6), the static view of humankind expressed here is surely his own. So, too, is the naive pseudo-anthropology. Coincidentally, the search for 'eternal principles' in primitive societies turns up results which, predictably, reinforce the need for imperial law and order, since imperialized territory could be seen as lacking either the evils of civilization or its blessings. Both views were ideologically sound. It was no fault of the observer, after all, if human nature revealed itself to an immoderate degree in murder, blood, and battle.

The special quality of romance which satisfied the needs of late-Victorian society, we may conclude, was its simple avowal of an existence of absolute truths which could pacify a large number of potentially disaffected people. These truths might be found, for example, in an escape to a remote locale, the implicit character of which recalls a time past and even an earlier stage of human development. Some of Haggard's historical romances thus 'rediscover' the harmony between humankind and nature, and explore cultures that appear to function on instinct and intuition. A similar kind of avowal of harmony can be found in the cult of the child and suggests itself in the writing both about and for boys. Romance tends to sentimentalize the African, the child, the past, and nature alike, creating images that perforce distort reality. It tends to distort reality in other ways as well: necessarily complex ideas are reduced to a base of universals while differences and distinctions are glossed over. Giving credibility to fundamental 'principles' of human nature, romance also aids the unified, classless and nationalistic society deemed necessary for imperial security.

The romance of Empire satisfied a desire for power, an obvious point, perhaps, but one that cannot be overlooked when so much of the realist and naturalist fiction of the period nullified power almost by definition. Andrew Lang gives some sense of the disdain in which this, to him depressing, fiction was held by the proponents of romance when he despaired at having to 'listen to the starved-mouse squeak in the *bouge* of Thérèse Raquin, with M. Zola' (1891, p. 4). Imperial romance made possible vicarious experiences of power. Their towering white soldiers or administrators controlled the indigenous populations of Africa or India. Technical expertise and bureaucratic know-how helped in this control, while an ineluctable charm also allowed the heroic imperialist to capture the prize woman, often partially if not wholly white. Quatermain always exhibits tremendous physical, psychological, and spiritual strength, which sustains him whether he is fighting an enemy, withstanding the torments of hunger, thirst, and pain, or battling wits with Ayesha. Yet Haggard's version of Everyman is sufficiently ordinary for most readers to identify themselves with, so the fantasy of power, quickly gratified in fictional confrontations with a primitive people, is easily indulged.

The idealization of Empire in both public oratory and literature is of a piece, as are other manifestations of this distortion of reality, such as the idealized images of boys, women, or Africans. Another example of this phenomenon is that writers of romance may view their own world through a series of distorting mirrors. Indeed, we can generalize from what T. S. Eliot said of George Wyndham, another imperialist and writer, in *The Sacred Wood* (1920): 'the world was an adventure of himself' (1964, p. 27). When Wyndham left for Egypt, according to Eliot, he wrote that, ' "we might have been Antony going to Egypt in a purple-sailed galley" ' (p. 27). Roger Lancelyn Green, in his biography of Andrew Lang, tells of a real treasure hunt in 1885 in which 'Lang, Haggard, and possibly Stevenson, were actually paying for shares' (1946, p. 112). As might be expected, then, romance is the sort of writing wherein the boundaries between writer and work are subject to collapse at any moment. Haggard has Quatermain make long-winded speeches that are nothing but pure Haggard, and his works are in fact a giant repository of his own attitudes. The formlessness that results from this sort of writing has the effect of creating a work with no end; nothing is self-contained, and the residue from the overflow, particularly in Haggard's fiction, turns out to be amateur philosophy at its worst. With all its apparent distance

33

from reality, romance does not distinguish itself as a separate, only more fanciful, world, but seems always to be arguing for a place in the affairs of every day.

As a literary term, romance is as difficult to define as its nearest kin, romanticism. The difficulty is due primarily to the fact that romance does not appear in a pure form anywhere. So-called 'realist' writers like Hardy, Gissing, and George Moore are prone to the idealization of certain scenes, passages, or whole characters in ways that are less than realistic. Even Zola's novels are full of the dynamism and impressionism that is associated with romantic flux and subjectivity. It is most practical, then, to speak of romance in relative terms, in terms of degree or tendency.

Romance is, to begin with, less than true to life, varying in gradation from writer to writer. Its world, according to Samuel Hynes in *Edwardian Occasions*, is 'rigged': 'Fictional romance alters the world as we know it, and creates in its place a "world-of-the-work" which is simpler, and less abrasive than our own, and which consequently appeals to the human will to escape (as the novel, presumably, appeals to our will to know)' (1972, p. 72). Edwin M. Eigner in *Robert Louis Stevenson and the Romantic Tradition* compares romance with realism and suggests that the realist 'finds the kernel of truth within his real or imagined experiences, while the writer of romance fabricates experience to illustrate a truth which in his vision or his theory he has already apprehended' (1964, p. 14). In the romance, experience does not reveal truth so much as validate it. For this reason, a lack of vigorous intellectual struggle, if not anti-intellectualism, prevails. Accordingly, romance exhibits a logical congeniality with messianic interpretations of Empire and with notions of ruling-class stability, both of which also depend upon *a priori* truths.

In addition to the fundamental idealism of romance, its imagined truths and its considerable indifference to literary verisimilitude, it possesses certain acknowledged conventions, most of which have been set out by Northrop Frye in his *Anatomy of Criticism*. Chief among them are the adventure plot and the quest or major adventure during which the hero often faces the enemy on a symbolically sterile and barren battlefield, which is later rejuvenated by the revivifying powers of the hero. Other features include descents into various species of the underworld, the buried treasure motif, and the presence of old wise men, magicians, or witches. The importance of romance in this discussion of Haggard and his milieu, however, is not its universal application, as is the case in Frye's *Anatomy*, but rather its specific application to a particular period and place in literary and political history.

No critique of romance could be more central to Haggard's period than that contained in Henry James's 'The art of fiction' and Stevenson's 'A humble remonstrance' (both 1884), two essays which debate the broad differences between the novel and the romance. The controversy between James and Stevenson turns on two points: one, the desirability of fictional classifications, and two, the desirability of realistic fiction. James is not interested in separate classifications but in a general and comprehensive order of fiction. Insisting on the integrity of description, incident, and dialogue in a fictional work, James is unsympathetic to the sort of criticism that treats these interrelated parts as if they existed 'in a series of blocks' (1968, p. 400). Such criticism, he suggests, leads to the marking of artificial fictional frontiers that are merely awkward critical crutches with little relevance for the writer:

The novel and the romance . . . [this clumsy separation appears] to have been made by critics and readers for their occasional predicaments, but to have little reality or interest for the producer, from whose point of view it is of course that we are attempting to consider the art of fiction.   (1968, p. 402)

For James, any undue emphasis on either character or incident would be a distortion of life, where character and incident are supporting elements, the one existing only because of the other. The 'only classification of the novel that I can understand', he writes, 'is into that which has life and that which has it not' (1968, p. 401). Presumably, the good novel may very well have elements of romance in it so long as these other elements have also drawn breath.

For Stevenson, on the other hand, romance encompasses more than fiction, and seems to be simply the art of narrative from the *Odyssey* through the *Canterbury Tales* to *The Lady of the Lake*. He divides fiction into three classes:

first, the novel of adventure, which appeals to certain almost sensual and quite illogical tendencies in man; second, the novel of character, which appeals to our intellectual appreciation of man's foibles and mingled and inconstant motives; and third, the dramatic novel . . . which appeals to our emotional nature and moral judgment.   (1947, p. 919)

Writers of fiction, Stevenson suggests, should alter their manner of writing accordingly: 'with each new subject . . . the true artist will vary his method and change the point of attack' (1947, p. 919).

The second issue of contention between James and Stevenson concerns the desirability of realistic fiction or fiction that is true to life. James writes that 'the only reason for the existence of a novel is that it does attempt to represent life' (1968, p. 389). So far as he is concerned, 'the air of reality (solidity of specification)' is 'the supreme virtue of a novel' (1968, p. 399). What James assumes is the writer's working intelligence, a mind that approaches the world with a view to understanding it, one that 'converts the very pulse of the air into revelations' (1968, p. 397).

Stevenson disagrees fundamentally. Life, which for James exists to be scrutinized, studied and analysed, is for Stevenson an overwhelming, thrilling immensity which refuses analysis or genuine comprehension:

Mr. James utters his mind with a becoming fervor on the sanctity of truth to the novelist; on a more careful examination truth will seem a word of very debatable propriety . . . No art – to use the daring word of Mr. James – can successfully 'compete with life.' . . . To 'compete with life', whose sun we cannot look upon, whose passion and diseases waste and slay us – to compete with the flavor of wine, the bitterness of death and separation – here is, indeed, a projected escalade of heaven.   (1947, pp. 917–18)

The very language of James and Stevenson reveals their differences, one sober and clear like the phrase 'solidity of specification', the other rhapsodical, sweeping, and passionate.

In 1887, just before going off to Egypt and Cyprus to gather material for *Cleopatra,* Haggard wrote his own defence of romance, 'About fiction', for the *Contemporary Review.* This article was apparently 'taken as a pendant to the controversy on the art of fiction' (Elwin, 1939, p. 248) carried on by James and Stevenson. Both imprudent and pretentious, 'About fiction' generated a series of attacks, led by W. T. Stead, on Haggard's own work. It begins with an outlandishly extravagant claim: 'the love of romance is probably coeval with the existence of humanity . . . In short, it is like the passions, an innate quality of mankind' (1887a, p. 172). Haggard then praised the romance writer with typical immodesty, suggesting that 'with the exception of perfect sculpture, really good romance writing is perhaps the most difficult art practised by the sons of men' (1887a, p. 173). Unlike either James or Stevenson, Haggard preferred ministering to his own ego rather than attending to the needs of aspiring writers:

The writer who can produce a noble and lasting work of art is of necessity a great man, and one who, had fortune opened to him any of the doors that lead to material grandeur and to the busy pomp of power, would have shown that the imagination, the quick sympathy, the insight, the depth of mind, and the sense of order and proportion which went to constitute the writer would have equally constituted the statesman or the general.   (1887a, p. 173)

Even in this confessional fantasy his political frame of reference is conveniently handy.

As for fiction offering anything like the Jamesian 'air of reality', such an idea seems never to have crossed Haggard's mind. Realistic fiction meant '[w]hatever there is brutal in humanity ... and whatever there is that is carnal and filthy' (1887a, p. 176). Such literature, Haggard lamented, neglects 'the great aspirations and the lofty hopes and longings, which do, after all, play their part in our human economy, and which it is surely the duty of a writer to call attention to and nourish according to his gifts' (1887a, p. 176). Calling for a higher ideal in English fiction, he speculated that, in the realm of pure imagination, we may 'cross the bounds of the known, and, hanging between earth and heaven, gaze with curious eyes into the great profound beyond' (1887a, p. 180). And when other types of fiction have had their day, Haggard predicted, romance, timeless and universal, will prevail: 'the kindly race of men in their latter as in their earlier developments will still take pleasure in those works of fancy which appeal, not to a class, or a nation, or even to an age, but to all time and humanity at large' (1887a, p. 180).

In his autobiography Haggard pronounced on matters of style and technique in romance writing, but the pronouncements are typically weak. 'Let the characters be definite, even at the cost of a little crudeness' (1926a, II, p. 92), he wrote, making a virtue of his own faults. 'Tricks of "style" and dark allusions may please the superior critic; they do not please the average reader' (1926a, II, p. 96). An overhasty and slapdash writer, he made speed another literary imperative for romancers: 'Again, such work should be written rapidly and, if possible, not rewritten, since wine of this character loses its bouquet when it is passed from glass to glass' (1926a, II, p. 92). Incident means action, and all is subordinate to movement: '[T]he story . . . should consist of action, action, action from the first page to the last. For the rest, little matters. Even if the writer does not know what is coming next the circumstance is of no importance, for it will come when it is wanted' (1926a, II, pp. 94–5). Details are secondary; the 'reader must help . . . out, must be the possessor of a certain receptive power and able to fill in a thousand minutiae of character and so forth, for to attempt to state these would overload the story' (1926a, II, p. 94). It was perhaps just as well that Haggard left his autobiography (and such discussions) for posthumous publication.

The differences between Haggard and Stevenson are plain. In Stevenson's hands the aesthetics of romance are more defensible and understandable. They are not only explained more articulately but more intelligently. At bottom, however, these two romancers share a sympathetic affinity, a similar retreat from details to abstractions, and an obsession with the colour and zest of life that exceeds an interest in understanding it. Self-professed romance writers appear to demand special regard as such.

While it is inevitable that the term 'romance' will continue to stimulate debate, some definition must be attempted which is inclusive enough to point to representative works and sufficiently open-ended to accommodate the possibility of variations. A sensible approach to this problem of definition is offered by Richard Chase in his 1957 essay, 'Novel vs. romance'. Beginning with a word of caution about trying to define the terms 'novel' and 'romance' too restrictively, he indentifies the major distinction between them as simply their manner of viewing reality. His lucid examination of this distinction follows:

The novel renders reality closely and in comprehensive detail. It takes a group of people and sets them going about the business of life. We come to see these people in the real complexity of their temperament and motive. They are in explicable relation to nature, to each other, to their social class, to their own past. Character is more important than action and plot, and probably the tragic or comic actions of the narrative will have the primary purpose of enhancing our knowledge of and feeling for an important character, a group of characters, or a way of life. The events that occur will usually be plausible, given the circumstances, and if the novelist includes a violent or sensational occurrence in his plot, he will introduce it only into such scenes as have been . . . 'already prepared to vouch for it'. . .

By contrast the romance . . . feels free to render reality in less volume and detail. It tends to prefer action to character, and action will be freer in a romance than in a novel, encountering, as it were, less resistance from reality. . . The romance can flourish without providing much intricacy of relation. The characters, probably rather two-dimensional types, will not be complexly related to each other or to society or to the past. Human beings will on the whole be shown in ideal relation – that is, they will share emotions only after these have become abstract or symbolic. To be sure, characters may become profoundly involved in some way . . . but it will be a deep and narrow, an obsessive, involvement . . . it will not matter much what class people come from, and where the novelist would arouse our interest in a character by exploring his origin, the romancer will probably do so by enveloping it in mystery. Character itself becomes, then, somewhat abstract and ideal, so much so in some romances that it seems to be merely a function of plot. The plot we may expect to be highly colored. Astonishing events may occur, and these are likely to have a symbolic or ideological, rather than a realistic plausibility. Being less committed to the immediate rendition of reality than the novel, the romance will more freely veer toward mythic, allegorical, and symbolistic forms.　　　　　　　　　　　　　　(Chase, 1969, pp. 282–3)

Chase's discursive analysis is not only jargon-free – there are no references to archetypes, mythic patterns, or the 'collective unconscious' – but it is also so obviously level-headed as to calm the uneasy opponents of literary classification. It maps out, so to speak, the terrain of fiction; and the charted areas, defined by contrast, sustain their distinctions by a tension of opposite forces exerting pressure on each other. The operative words are detail, complexity, plausibility, and motivation. We can speak of more or less detail, more or less complexity, more or less plausibility, or more or less motivation. The relative strength of these forces allows us to refer to a romance as focusing more on action than character, the inexplicable world than the explicable, discontinuity of experience than its continuity.

Chase's definition perhaps ought to be modified in one respect, that is, its statement regarding class. Indeed, experience in romance generally has less to do with people as social products than as isolated individuals. But a dismissal of class is more applicable to American literature, Chase's special area, with its pervasive and intensely felt myth of a classless society, than to British literature. For the romances of Haggard, a more accurate statement would be: 'it does not matter what class people come from so long as they stay in it'. Haggard's romances are dependent upon a class society, albeit a harmonious one. Although Allan Quatermain and his companions are characterized as ordinary men who speak plainly, act spontaneously, and represent a type of Englishman and an example of decency, a hierarchical ordering of life is a given of their world.

Types, or ideals – essential to romance – help to contribute to notions of race and nation, minimizing the significance of class differences. Such characterization, no matter how suitable to the literary form, simultaneously smooths over and supports class differences. Quatermain always takes note of the class stratification of the various African nations he encounters, suggesting that social stratification is universal. In *Allan Quatermain*, for example, the people of Milosis are dressed according to their social standing, togas being 'of different shades of colour, from white to deepest brown, according to the rank of the wearer' (Haggard, 1919a, p. 158). The people are 'divided into great classes as in civilized countries' with the 'best bred people' being pure and white and the 'common herd' darker (1919a, p. 175). Similarly, in *Child of Storm*, Quatermain reassures readers that the Zulus 'have a social system not unlike our own. They have, or had, their kings, their nobles, and their commons' (Haggard, 1952, p. 74).

The central point of Chase's discussion, drawn from James's Preface to *The American*, is that the 'disconnected and uncontrollable experience' is the heart of romance. For James, the phrase 'disconnected and uncontrollable experience' described a certain part of *The American* which he saw to be illustrative of romance writing. Chase concludes with James's statement from the Preface which elaborates the nature of this experience:

The only *general* attribute of projected romance that I can see, the only one which fits all of its cases, is the fact of the kind of experience with which it deals – experience liberated, so to speak; experience disengaged, disembroiled, disencumbered, exempt from the conditions that we usually know to attach to it, and, if we wish so to put the matter drag upon it, and operating in a medium which relieves it, in a particular interest, of the inconvenience of a *related*, a measurable state, a state subject to all our vulgar communities.

(James, 1970, p. xviii)

Experience in romance is, in sum, inexplicable, incoherent, and discontinuous. Forces beyond fact, beyond the phenomenal world, direct and shape it. We can proceed by custom, by tradition, by instinct, or blindly, but we can never make coherent sense of the whole. Thus, whatever path the examination of romance turns up, there is always a way back to idealism.

In the imperial romance, the liberated experience to which James refers is implicit not only in the adventure-story formula but in characterization; both are equally free of the restraints of the ordinary world. For Haggard, the quintessential Englishman was an adventurer, the 'free man' in stereotype. This was certainly not a new classification for men who had ruled the seas since the seventeenth century, but it did have a new imperial twist. Quatermain contends that 'Englishmen are adventurers to the backbone; and all our muster-roll of colonies, each of which will in time become a great nation, testify to the extraordinary value of the spirit of adventure' (Haggard, 1919a, p. 114). As for Quatermain's definition of an adventurer, he is a man 'who goes out to meet whatever may come . . . [with a] brave heart and a trust in Providence' (1919a, p. 114). The Christian knight is supplanted by the enterprising imperial hero.

Freedom itself, however, is not an unqualified good. Stevenson's *Dr. Jekyll and Mr. Hyde* (1886) reveals an ambivalence to freedom common to many romances. Hyde, a total egomaniac, is a veritable 'sea of liberty' (Stevenson, 1968, p. 52). Stevenson's *Treasure Island* (1883) exhibits a similarly ambivalent attitude to freedom with its dramatization of the rebellious and free-wheeling Long John Silver, while his *Weir of Hermiston* (1896) is complicated by a much subtler treatment of rebellion and freedom in the relationship between Archie Weir and his domineering father. In Kipling, aimless freedom brings on the threat of anarchy in both the *Jungle Books* (1894–5) and *Kim* (1901), but probably the most disturbing example of this ambivalent attitude to freedom occurs in Kenneth Grahame's *The Wind in the Willows* (1908), when Rat is persuaded to overcome his temptation to follow the sea-faring rat away from the river. For Haggard, the sort of anarchic freedom that troubled Kipling was identified as an attribute of the Boer. Unlike Stevenson and Grahame, Haggard and Kipling travelled, lived, and worked in the Empire and had a more politically defined sense of freedom and its limits.

To return briefly to the question of character types, romancers generally present abstractions rather than individuals, the hero being the ideal to which the reader is supposed to aspire. In Haggard's romances, Quatermain is 'the hunter', Umslopogaas 'the warrior', and Ayesha 'the immortal woman'. Two, three, or even four characters may appear as abstractions of a whole. In *King Solomon's Mines* Haggard's Gagool is pure evil while Foulata is pure good; in *Allan Quatermain* the fair Nyleptha is opposed by the dark Sorais; in *Child of Storm* the generous Mbulazi battles the mean-spirited Cetshwayo; and in *The World's Desire* Helen and Meriamun represent sacred and profane love. National types – or rather stereotypes – appear as well. Alphonse in *Allan Quatermain* is a comic and cowardly Frenchman. The Portuguese are always 'the slavers'. Germans are never to be trusted. The black, the Boer, and the Jew are also formulaic types, and within their own classifications hardly distinguishable. Haggard has succeeded very well in making his characters 'definite at the cost of crudeness'.

More important than character is action, the central experience in romance and the strongest link between romance and the imperial world. This action, as a rule, is also 'liberated', as James would say, from the restraints of such things as family and job. Quatermain's wife and son are dead; Ludwig Holly of *She* and *Ayesha* is a bachelor; Leo Vincey's father conveniently dies at the beginning of *She*; Umslopogaas is estranged from his people, as is Umbopa or Ignosi in *King Solomon's Mines* (although he is restored as chief in the end). In fact, Hannah Arendt's remarks on Kipling's *Kim* can be applied generally to Haggard's romances and a host of other works of the same type: 'Life itself seems to be left in a fantastically intensified purity, when man has cut himself off from all ordinary social ties, family, regular occupation, a definite goal, ambitions, and the guarded place in the community to which he belongs by birth' (1958, p. 217). The absence of a definite goal, a feature of many of Haggard's romances, might appear to distance a particular tale from Empire. In effect, however, it feeds the idea that whatever is created by the British protagonist is the inevitable result of what destiny has flung in his way. By virtue of his adventurous spirit and hard work, he bravely faces whatever comes and transforms it into a good on the spot, spontaneously and unobtrusively.

In *King Solomon's Mines*, the active life is tied to duty and responsibility only peripherally; that is, Curtis's search for his lost brother is merely a frame for the adventure. The action proper concerns the treasure of the mines, and the treasure hunt almost immediately supersedes the original search. Once the Kukuanas appear and the dual source of evil is identified in Twala, the one-eyed king, and in Gagool, the witch, then duty, responsibility, and honour reappear in full dress as Quatermain and his friends return the rightful heir to the throne and rid the land of Twala and Gagool. As always, the Englishmen are good sports, react spontaneously in the face of adversity, combat evil, and restore order.

The same kind of spontaneous action occurs in *Allan Quatermain*, in which the framing motive for adventure is simply escape from civilization. This time Quatermain and his friends, along with Umslopogaas, wrest the Zu Vendis from the hands of some superstitious, power-hungry priests and Queen Sorais. As always, the Englishmen are presented as men who never initiate trouble but can be counted on to struggle through to the end when it appears. They fight only in self-defence, as Quatermain repeatedly tells the blood-lusty Umslopogaas, but they fight to win.

As their readers might be led to expect, Haggard and his fellow literary imperialists privately held the activist views that pervade their publications. To Haggard the writing of fiction was itself too sedentary and paled in comparison with the business of dutiful struggles, outdoor exercise, and general physical activity. In the 1890s he said that he 'wearied of fiction and longed for the life of action to which [he] had been bred and that, indeed, [was] native to [his] character' (1926a, II, p. 86). Action as work was linked for him with the idea of service: 'To me happiness and work well done, or service faithfully accomplished, are words with a like meaning' (1926a, II, p. 89). The most intensely felt need for personal activism was probably expressed by Robert Louis Stevenson and W. E. Henley, both of whom were physically unable to enjoy the strenuous life they advocated, although Stevenson made a fair try. The Stevenson of 'Aes Triplex' in *Virginibus Puerisque* (1881) declared that there was 'but one conclusion possible: that a man should stop his ears against the paralysing terror, and run the race that is set before him with a single mind' (1911, p. 110). This is the culmination of the Victorian work ethic – Tennyson and Browning diluted to pithy maxims. 'To travel hopefully is a better thing than to arrive', Stevenson wrote in 'El Dorado', 'and the true success is to labour' (1911, p. 120).

'Invictus' and the 'In Hospital' poems make clear Henley's resolve for a physical and active life, as does his frequent use of the *carpe diem* motif in other poetry. In 'Pro Rege Nostro', the personal devotion to activism is converted to a public song of service in action. In the case of Kipling the examples are too numerous to cite, 'Tomlinson' being perhaps the clearest, with its ' "Ye have read, ye have heard, ye have thought", he said, and the tale is yet to run:/"By the worth of the body that once ye had, give answer – what ha' ye done?" '(1919, p. 412). From the explicitly imperial point of view there is 'The White Man's Burden', another call for strenuous, bracing activity; 'take up' the burden, he advised Americans, and in this way 'search your manhood' (1919, p. 327). Again, the uncertain nature of the goal in this poem is cause for attention. As David Daiches aptly remarked in *Some Late Victorian Attitudes*, 'When in 1899 [Kipling] urged the United States to take up the White Man's Burden in the Philippines he did not claim that it was for the sake of the Filipinos – it was in order to test the white man's endurance and give him a strenuous work-out' (1969, p. 19).

Among the conclusions to be drawn from our examination of romance so far, the most significant is that romance, by virtue of its immunity to the ties of actuality, is a literary form characterized by freedom and expansiveness. These two attributes of romance suggest a natural kinship not only between romance and the geographical immensity of the imperial world, but also between romance and the mood of imperial Britain as a whole, reacting against the restraints of markets, tariffs and competitive nation-states. Romance characters can be set free from place, time, or history whenever their authors are so inclined. In Haggard's writings the restraints of time are subverted by any number of rebirths, doubles, reincarnations, or returns to former lives. Benita de Ferreira, the daughter of a Portuguese sea captain, speaks three hundred years later through the medium of a Victorian Benita; Allan Quatermain returns to the Ice Age in *The Ancient Allan*; an interval of a mere two hundred and fifty thousand years exists for two of the characters in *When the World Shook*; and Ayesha's immortality is well known. History, age, and time are the drags on experience, the restrictions that romance can overcome.

Another possibility for romance, also dependent on the freedom of its form, is its ideological plasticity. It can be controlled and manipulated so easily that it can be made to do the romancer's

44

ideological bidding. The allegorical nature of romance has an infinite capacity for political propagandizing. Haggard's romances, even when not explicit propaganda for Empire, often contain political (especially militaristic) allusions. As Kipling once said, Haggard is 'a whale at parables and allegories and one thing reflecting another' (Haggard, Lilias Rider, 1951, p. 272). Often, in the least imaginative of Haggard's works, the reflecting devices offer little more than dull bits of conventional clichés and commonplaces as the political idealism of Empire throws back the most banal of images. But the anxieties of the imperial age, especially the fear of war – European, civil, or colonial – are reflected too in the most compelling of Haggard's stories. Thus, while the reflection of imperial idealism is surely the imperialist's stock-in-trade, the reflection of anxiety and indecision – in so far as it captures the disordered psyche of the age – has more suggestive implications.

In Haggard's early fiction, that is, fiction before the turn of the century and the Boer War, this amorphous political anxiety may be discerned in his out-and-out African adventures like *King Solomon's Mines*, *Allan Quatermain*, and *Nada the Lily*. In these otherwise simple adventure stories, Haggard shows first of all his keen interest in military defensiveness. The Zulus, along with other African nations, exhibited a military strength that sparked Haggard's enthusiasm and admiration, and he consciously presented their militarism as somewhat extreme, but on the whole thoroughly splendid. In *King Solomon's Mines*, he brings home the relevance of their militarism by introducing Germany into the African context. 'Indeed', says Quatermain, 'in Kukuanaland, as among the Germans, the Zulus, and the Masai, every able-bodied man is a soldier, so that the whole force of the nation is available for its wars, offensive or defensive' (Haggard, 1955, p. 115). He is clearly impressed by the effectiveness of the Kukuana army, with its 'perfect discipline and steady unchanging valour' (1955, p. 180). The citing of Germany as a European point of reference is obviously intentional. The same parallel between the Zulus and the Germans is made in *Cetywayo*, where Haggard describes the Zulu military system as the 'universal-service system of Germany brought to an absolute perfection, obtained by subordinating all the ties and duties of civil life to military ends' (1896, p. 21).

In the post-Boer War period Haggard made much stronger allusions to military preparedness in two particular romances, *Ayesha* (1905) and *Queen Sheba's Ring* (1910). At this time the perceived threats of degeneracy from within and invasion from without were intensified, due mainly to military humiliations suffered during the Boer War, German domination of South West Africa, German designs on Delagoa Bay on Africa's eastern coast, and a general strain on Anglo-German relations. Moreover, Haggard's sense of the degeneration of the race and its attendant lack of military consciousness made decadence a prime target for attack.

In the earlier work, *Ayesha*, the presentation of an effete ruling class was meant to be a clear warning that Britain should act, work, and regain its vitality. The Khania of Kaloon, one of Haggard's many female rulers, is disgusted by her court and its idleness, and she accurately predicts the downfall of her people. The implied criticism of Haggard's fellow countrymen in the Khania's following harangue is directed at well-fed but indifferent materialists: 'Swine will to their mire and these men and women, who live in idleness upon the toil of the humble folk, will to their liquor and vile luxury. Well, the end is near, for it is killing them, and their children are but few; weakly also, for the ancient blood grows thin and stale' (Haggard, 1905, p. 104).

Queen Sheba's Ring, an extended allegory on degeneracy and an insistent and contrived prompting to military awareness, aims to arouse fear by concentrating on the sad fate of a nation of Abyssinian Jews, the Abati, the putative children of Solomon and Sheba. The notions of war and battle in this tale demand no intellectual sophistication on the part of the reader, appealing primarily to a non-critical audience affected by easily understood messages and object-lessons. Like so much of Haggard's fiction, *Queen Sheba's Ring* is narrated in the first person, an easy way to minimize objectivity and to intrude with authorial comment. Richard Adams, a one-time doctor and lifelong adventurer with, predictably, 'no strict ties at home' (Haggard, 1965b, p. 9), persuades the well-known antiquarian Professor Ptolemy Higgs to join in the rescue of Adams's son, who has been kept as a slave for about twelve years by a North African people called the Fung. Adams promises the aid of the last descendant of the Queens of Sheba, the Walda Nagasta (meaning Child of Kings), who is trying to withstand attacks from the Fung with her weak and degenerate Abati people. The plan is to destroy the god of the Fung by means of explosives. According to legend, the people will follow this symbolic demise of their nation by dispersing, thus freeing Adams's son and ridding the Abati of their mortal enemies. During his interview with the eccentric papyrus-reading Higgs, Adams is introduced to Oliver Orme, a former officer in the Boer War, and Sergeant Quick, Orme's servant, who has also served against the Boers. Both men are obvious military assets; moreover, Orme is coincidentally an engineer capable of handling explosives. They are invited to join the expedition, which gets underway at once.

After a great deal of gratuitous adventure, including a lion hunt and a life-threatening desert sandstorm, the journey proper begins, and the Englishmen proceed to the mountain fortress of the Abati. The trip takes them through dangerous Fung territory where they are hunted by menacing horsemen. Higgs is eventually taken prisoner by the Fung while the other three, trapped in the city of Harmac and facing outrageous odds, terrify the Fung by firing their rifles and detonating a mine. (Orme later calls this intimidation unsportsman-like but necessary.) By diverting their would-be attackers, the Englishmen finally make their escape, and at the end of their flight they meet the Walda Nagasta, also called Maqueda, and her cavalry.

With the entrance of the Abati, Haggard begins his pointed inferences about weak military consciousness. Orme suggests that the Maqueda's cavalry should take advantage of the moment when their enemies are most vulnerable to launch an attack, but the Abati, 'a nation of curs' (1965b, p. 125) with 'no idea of discipline' (p. 91), are unwilling to fight. Their ruler, who is understandably impressed with the English and their bravery and 'was known always to have been in favour of conscription and perfect readiness to repel attack' (p. 180), is ashamed of her people. She refuses Orme's advice with the explanation that her 'people are not – war-like' (p. 80). What they are is extravagant, indulgent, and immodest, a people content with speaking of their past glories rather than accepting their present responsibilities.

The Fung are clearly meant to suggest a likeness to the Germans. They are manifestly able warriors and they esteem heroism in others as well. When an envoy of peaceful emissaries comes from the Fung who, by the way, 'hem in' Abati trade, its leader, Barung, lavishes admiration upon the English and their heroic tradition, going so far as to include a reference to Gordon in his recognition of their famous military exploits: 'I have heard of you English before – Arabs and traders brought me tales of you. For instance, there was one who died defending a city against a worshipper of the Prophet . . . down yonder at Khartoum on the Nile – a great death, they told me . . . which your people avenged afterwards' (p. 88). Countering this image of the heroic English soldier, however, is a critique of the civilian population which appeared grossly inappreciative of the military community. Sergeant Quick remembers the silence that greeted him 'after being left for dead on Spion Kop with a bullet through my lung and mentioned in a dispatch' (p. 94). Failure to understand the importance of military preparedness leaves the English at great risk. The fictional Fung, on the other hand, ensure that 'every [Fung] man was trained to war' (p. 180).

The Abati, it seems, suffer from the same debilitating philosophy that Haggard claimed afflicted the Liberals of his day – a misplaced humanism, a penchant for ease, and a degenerate morality. This is apparent in Maqueda's explanation of why all Abati men do not bear arms:

'In the old days it was otherwise, when my great ancestors ruled, and then we did not fear the Fung. But now the people will not serve as soldiers. They say it takes them from their trades and the games they love; they say they cannot give the time in youth; they say that it degrades a man to obey the orders of those set over him; they say that war is barbarous and should be abolished, and all the while the brave Fung wait without to massacre our men and make our women slaves. Only the very poor and the desperate, and those who have offended against the laws will serve in my army, except it be as officers . . . therefore the Abati are doomed.' (p. 108)

To Haggard, these were pacifist, materialist, even democratic, ideas which weakened and divided; they were therefore hateful and offensive.[1] When Adams hears Maqueda's speech, he is sickened by the 'utter degeneracy of the race she was called upon to rule' (p. 108). Soon after, Haggard drags in his other *bête noir*, the failure to store agricultural produce against the days of invasion. The Abati do not save enough corn and they refuse to contribute to the public store. 'And yet a day may come', Adams says, 'when a store of corn alone would stand between them and death by hunger – if the Fung held the valley, for instance' (p. 113).

In this way the message gradually becomes clear: although the Abati have a great historic legacy, they have no immediate strength, and they are a doomed people. Much like Kipling's 'The Islanders', they are a smug and confident people, indifferent to external danger because of their being an isolated island nation. It is precisely this false sense of security that will cause them to neglect the threat of invasion regardless, says Adams, of periodic threats of an invasion over many years:

From their childhood they had heard of the imminence of invasion, but no actual invasion had ever yet taken place. The Fung were always without, and they were always within, an inland isle, the wall of rock that they thought impassable being their sea which protected them from danger.   (p. 166)

In the event that some imperceptive reader might fail to notice the alarm bells going off, Haggard then appends the following remarks to an incident in which the Abati are terrified by the invading Fung:

It was as though we English learned that a huge foreign army had suddenly landed on our shores and, having cut the wires and seized the railways, was marching upon London. The effect of such tidings upon a nation that always believed invasion to be impossible may easily be imagined, only I hope that we should take them better than did the Abati.   (p. 179)[2]

The Fung naturally overrun the Abati, who are to become their slaves; and Maqueda, who might have saved the day, leaves her people to their fate with the following judgement:

'If you had listened to me and to those whom I called in to help us, you might have beaten back the Fung, and remained free for ever. But you were cowards; you would not learn to bear arms like men, you would not even watch your mountain walls, and soon or late the people who refuse to fight must fall and become the servants of those who are ready.'   (p. 256)

The association of cowardice, luxury, and pleasure in the Abati underlines the ascetic and spartan character of Haggard's activism. And asceticism brings together the activism of Haggard's straight-forward adventure stories and that of his decidedly more spiritual works. Often a way to moral regeneration, action involves a denial of personal wants and becomes a moral code. The plain adventure stories and the spiritual romances like *She* (1887), *The World's Desire* (1890), *Ayesha* (1905), and *Wisdom's Daughter* (1923) are two sides of one highly inflated anti-materialist and idealist coin. In the spiritual tales, the quest is for universal unity; life on earth is merely a fragmented, divided path which one travels on the way to unification with God, or the One, or an idea, or some universal force. The link between these otherworldly books and the rip-roaring adventures is

49

the idea of self-abnegation. And sacrifice, in turn, nourishes the notion of service.

As a literary form, then, romance accommodates itself to the politics of imperialism, the didacticism being implicit in the form. Yet Haggard succeeded in using romance as an even more powerful vehicle of imperial ideology by incorporating in it either tangential or whole arguments generated by imperial concerns. Running through most of Haggard's work is the connecting thread of his philosophical world-view, an abstract notion of politics and Empire that was occasionally difficult, even for Haggard, to reconcile with the facts of the imperial world. His imperial vision, to begin with, was messianic in conception, at least as far back as 1877 when he wrote his essay on 'The Transvaal': 'We Englishmen', he asserted, 'came to this land . . . with "a high mission of truth and civilization." ' . . . It is our mission to conquer and hold in subjection, not from thirst of conquest, but for the sake of law, justice, and order' (1877b, pp. 78–9). Later, in an 1898 address to a meeting of the Anglo–African Writers' Club, he assumed the pseudo-democratic posture of social-imperialism: 'I do not believe in the divine right of kings, but I do believe . . . in a divine right of a great civilising people – that is, in their divine mission' (Cohen, 1965, p. 35). This mission to conquer, which he believed divine in theory, was annoyingly human in fact; and Haggard was to be disappointed repeatedly by the blighting hand of reality. These threats to Empire came from government policy and from what he perceived as the prevailing materialist spirit that afflicted his society. Both furnished him with a wide field for critical attack, yielding political messages that take the form of diatribes against unpatriotic and anti-imperial elements in England.

Haggard's disappointment with English society was particularly strong in the eighties and nineties when, still fresh from the South African veld, he was almost totally preoccupied by Gladstone's policies in the Transvaal. His fictional response to Gladstone's government, which is contained in *The Witch's Head, Jess, Colonel Quaritch, V.C., The Way of the Spirit*, and probably the original version of *She* (Cohen, 1968, p. 182), gave way later to less strident attacks when, for one thing, the fear of invasion from Germany superseded in its urgency the South African situation and, for another, he turned his mind to agriculture. What is significant about these early works is their presentation of the voice of the moribund gentry and the way the imperial landscape lent itself to the diffusion of sentimental pastoral impulses. Haggard's attraction to Empire was based partly on a reaction to the forces of free trade, Liberalism, and industrialization – ironically, all that had made Empire possible – which were eroding the landowning tradition and changing the face of England. The central targets of his hostility were Radical Liberalism and commercialism.

In his first work, *Dawn* (1884), a melodrama of country life, Haggard refers to the South African situation peripherally in a passage which is designed to call attention to the callousness of the Liberal government. A thoroughly unprincipled Gladstonian, Lord Minster, recounts a shipboard experience en route to Madeira which exposes his total indifference to human suffering. A fellow voyager, he says, who 'had been ruined by the retrocession of the Transvaal, and [had heard] that I was in the Government, took every possible opportunity to tell me publicly that his wife and children were almost in a state of starvation, as though I cared about his confounded wife and children' (Haggard, 1887b, p. 226). In addition to this perverse insensitivity, Minster displays the unscrupulous character of the 'party' man, describing the science of government as 'knowing how to get into office, and remain there when once in' (1887b, p. 222). Patriotism, he suggests, is a relic of the past:

'all the old-fashioned Jingo nonsense about patriotism and the 'honour of the country' has, if people only knew it, quite exploded; it only lingers in a certain section of the landed gentry and a proportion of the upper middle class, and has no serious weight with leading politicians'.   (1887b, p. 222)

As with so many of Haggard's characters, Lord Minster is the embodiment of an idea, in this case Radicalism. To avoid any misinterpretation of the term, Haggard has Minster spell out the deliberately manipulative and corrupt nature of his party:

'The instinct of robbery is perhaps the strongest in human nature, and those who would rule humanity on its present basis must pander to it or fail. The party of progress means the party that can give the most spoil, taken, from those who have, to those who have not. That is why Mr. Gladstone is such a truly great man; he understands better than anyone of his age how to excite the greed of hungry voters and to guide it for his own ends . . . The Liberal party, or rather the Radical section, which is to the great Liberal party what the helm is to the ship, appeals to the baser instincts and more pressing appetites of the people; the Conservative only to their traditions and higher aspirations, in the same way that religion appeals to the spirit, and worship of Mammon to the senses. The shibboleth of one is "self-interest", of the other, "national honor". The first appeals to the many, the second to the finer few, and I must leave you to judge which will carry the day.' (1887b, pp. 222–3)

The polarizing of Liberals – or Radicals – and Conservatives on the basis of their supposed materialist and idealist characters is a commonplace of Haggard's fiction.

In *Jess* (1887), Haggard took the opportunity to attack Gladstone's policies during the first Boer War, which had culminated in the defeat at Majuba Hill. *Jess* is a largely fictional version of *Cetywayo*, dramatizing the plight of the British in the Transvaal during the retrocession. Old Farmer Crofts, who is initially undisturbed by rumours of a Boer rebellion, believes the British will never give up the Transvaal and says as much to an insurgent Boer: 'What did General Wolseley say the other day at the dinner at Potchefstroom? Why, that the country would never be given up, because no government, Conservative, Liberal, or Radical, would dare to do such a thing' (Haggard, 1889a, pp. 94–5). When he is eventually taken prisoner by the Boers, all trust in his country is destroyed, and he regards himself as a victim of British treachery: 'England has deserted us and I have no country' (p. 229). Earlier in the book his more perceptive niece Jess cautions her unsuspecting sister to treat an unwelcome Boer suitor with particular care: 'The other people are in power now in England, and one does not know what they may do . . . They might give us up to the Boers. You must remember that we far-away people are only the counters with which they play their game' (p. 50). The sister, like her mistaken uncle, insists that 'Englishmen are not like that. When they say a thing, they stick to it' (p. 51). Jess warns her bitterly that such honesty is a thing of the past.[3]

A better understanding of the nature of Haggard's critique in *Jess* may be had by referring to *Cetywayo*, in which his major concerns were the vital necessity of the inviolability of the British word and what he saw as the deplorable and almost treasonous break with duty and responsibility on the part of Gladstone. He was shocked, for example, that Garnet Wolseley's promise not to return Cetshwayo to rule the Zulus was thrown aside by the Liberals as was his promise that the Transvaal would remain a British possession.[4] These broken promises, in Haggard's view, undermined the honour, the integrity, and ultimately the security of the Empire. That Haggard's pleas for

British honour and integrity were implicit arguments for real power is not beside the point.

Besides attacking Gladstonian policy during the first Boer War, *Jess* also opens fire upon English commercialism, the spirit-destroying force, for Haggard, in late nineteenth-century England. The charges against commercialism are voiced by an old Boer and reveal Haggard's limited understanding of the changing British economy:

'The Englishman . . . understands his shop; he is buried in his shop, and can think of nothing else. Sometimes he goes away and starts his shop in other places, and buries himself in it, and makes it a big shop, because he understands shops. But it is all a question of shops, and if the shops abroad interfere with the shops at home, or if it is thought that they do, which comes to the same thing, then the shops at home put an end to the shops abroad. Bah! they talk a great deal there in England, but, at the bottom of it, it is shop, shop, shop. They talk of honor and patriotism too, but they both give way to the shop.'   (1889a, p. 153)

It is not unusual for Haggard to have put this criticism into the mouth of a Boer, for the Boers, as much as Haggard disliked them, had for him a quality of rough honesty which came from their relative freedom from contamination by the moneyed society of merchant capitalism. This sort of speech fits not only the sentiments of a Boer farmer, however, but those of Englishmen in later books, like De la Molle in *Colonel Quaritch, V.C.* (1888) and Alan Vernon in *The Yellow God* (1909), men who could not bear to rub elbows with the merchant class. Its sneering tone is that of a man who is momentarily vexed as distinct from one who is genuinely angry, for it is the pettiness of capitalism that Haggard seems to have despised, and, because he appears to have seen only its pettiness, he failed to see its power. Surely the idea of England as a nation of shopkeepers was hardly applicable to Rhodes's Charter Company and had little to do with the Empire Haggard knew.

An equally virulent attack on commerce, this time on business and banks, is launched in *Colonel Quaritch, V.C.*, a nostalgic work which dwells sentimentally on the nobility of the English gentry and reveals a profound longing for an idyllic sort of feudalism. Haggard presents us with the antagonistic personalities of Edward Cossey, 'the man of business', and Squire De la Molle, 'the gentleman of family'. The banker Cossey, for whom money is the pervading principle of life, is the socially and morally inferior villain of the piece. The superior De la Molle, on the other hand, is the kind of Englishman to whom 'this country owes her greatness' (Haggard, 1888, p. 92). His is a breed known for 'manliness, for downright English, godfearing virtues, for love of queen, country, family, and home' (1888, p. 329). The victim of greedy bankers like Cossey, De la Molle is almost forced to give his old estate up to the auction block. Respect for family and for the past is gone, and the banks sell up any number of old families for a price: 'the present is strictly a commercial age' (1888, p. 65), we are reminded again and again, and 'competition [a Liberal theme] and Radical agitation have brought estates down more than people realize' (1888, p. 64). The familiar attack on Liberals and Radicals is here accompanied by an implicit criticism of their free trade policies, driving home to Haggard's readership once again the injuries done to the agricultural sector of the economy.

In 1898 Haggard published *Dr Therne*, yet another assault on Radicalism and its dishonesty. Dr Therne's Radical benefactor, who wants him to support such things as a graduated income tax, old age pensions, and anti-vaccination, persuades the doctor to run for parliament as a Radical on an anti-vaccinationist platform with which he personally disagrees. The suggestion throughout this short book is that Radicals knowingly exploit ignorant people, and Therne himself admits that he 'sold ... [his] honour to win a seat in Parliament' (Haggard, 1898, p. 235). When Dr Therne's daughter contracts smallpox, he vaccinates himself; and the daughter, who witnesses this last act of deception, dies. Her lover is left to expose Therne as a fraud.

This attitude towards Radicals appears unchanged a short while later in *The Way of the Spirit* (1906). Haggard's definition of a Radical here is one who 'wished to pull down and burn for the sake of the crash and the flare' (1906, p. 151). Set against Dick Learmer, the Radical scoundrel of the book, is Rupert Ullershaw, the Liberal Imperialist or Unionist – it is not clear which, but an attempt to portray new trends in Liberalism is tried. The lesson to be learned from Ullershaw is that imperialists, faced with difficulties in foreign lands and a lack of understanding in their own, get better and better, deepen their spiritual awareness, and die for grand ideals. When Haggard describes Ullershaw, he is simultaneously describing the imperialist's creed: Ullershaw is an Imperialist, believing in the mission of Britain among the peoples of the earth, and desiring the consolidation of her empire's might because it meant justice, peace, and individual security; because it freed the slave, paralysed the hands of rapine, and caused the corn to grow and the child to laugh.

(1906, p. 151)

The Empire presented here is a phenomenon beyond accountability. No one need appeal to any actual concept of justice, peace, or security because the Empire is, tautologically, justice, peace, and security, and it appeals to nothing greater than itself.

In *The Yellow God*, Alan Vernon is a younger version of Squire De la Molle. When the book opens, he has just left his post in West Africa, having served as a major in the army, to save his failing estate in England. Vernon gets himself involved with a bunch of shady financiers, but extricates himself from the situation honourably enough (for Haggard) by going back to Africa to steal the god of a tribe that worships gold. Like *Colonel Quaritch*, *The Yellow God* would have it that bankers, financiers, and shady money lenders are distinct from the Empire itself, wild aberrations on the imperial scene and enemies of the imperial forces represented by the good old stock of Alan Vernon. It is clear that Haggard's understanding of imperialism, or at least his portrayal of it, is somewhat imperfect. His constant efforts to divest Empire of any material base show either a gross and deliberate oversight of economic reality or a naive but willing disbelief in the activities of imperial profiteers.

The subordination of material to spiritual elements in Empire sounds remarkably like Milner and, in fact, Haggard shared with Milner and other 'principled' imperialists (his friend Kipling, for one) a mistrust of two particular aspects of government we normally associate with democracy: majority representation and the party system. Both of these, Haggard suggested, divided and weakened British power, and thus countered the vital consolidating task of Empire. In the political history *Cetywayo*, Haggard expressed his disapproval of representative government in the Cape Colony, for example, arguing that, 'When, in our mania for representative institutions, we thrust responsible government upon the Cape, we placed ourselves practically at the mercy of any chance anti-English majority' (1896, p. lxviii). Disregarding the will of the majority was apparently the lesser evil. The party system is implicitly disparaged in every criticism of Radicalism. It is most strongly attacked in *The Way of the Spirit*, where it is described as a system that encourages shady dealing by the parties jockeying for power. The imperialist Ullershaw, who fails to carry out an imperial mission because of truly insurmountable obstacles, is totally discredited because of all sorts of insinuations made against him 'for party purposes' (Haggard, 1906, p. 220). *Marie* (1912), a retelling of the Great Trek of 1836, suggests that it was the party system that caused the Boers to suffer at the hands of the English in the early nineteenth century, when parties 'played strange tricks with the interests of political dependencies' (Haggard, 1912, p. 64). Haggard feared that under the party system, the imperial movement was likely to become the plaything of party interests.

Coupled with his distrust of the party system was Haggard's more general distrust or dislike of all governmental machinery and particularly the expanding bureaucracy of the nineteenth century. In *Jess*, the heroic rescue of the heroine by John Neil gave Haggard the chance to deliver one of his longer discourses on the instinctive soundness of the British national character, shown here to be threatened by an emasculating bureaucracy. John Neil's decisive and wilful character brings forth the following passage:

It is wonderful how far a mood of this sort will take a man. Indeed, it is the widespread possession of this sentiment that has made England what she is. Now it is beginning to die down and be legislated out of our national character, and the results are already commencing to appear in the incipient decay of our power. We can not govern Ireland. It is beyond us; let Ireland have Home Rule! We can not cope with our Imperial responsibilities; let them be cast off; and so on. The Englishman of fifty years ago did not talk like this. Well, every nation becomes emasculated sooner or later, that seems to be the universal fate; and it appears that it is our lot to be emasculated, not by the want of law, but by a plethora of it. This country was made, not by governments, but mostly in despite of them by the independent efforts of a series of individuals. The tendency nowadays is to merge the individual in the government, and to limit and even forcibly destroy personal enterprise and responsibility. Everything is to be legislated for or legislated against. The system is only in its bud as yet. When it blooms the empire will lose touch of its individual atoms and become a vast soulless machine, which will first get out of order, then break down, and, last of all, break up.

(Haggard, 1889a, p. 110)

Personal will struggles with the political machine. As Haggard saw things, individual effort was the way to prevent the dissolution of Empire.

Haggard expressed no desire for checks on power by either opposition parties or the public. The absence of any such desire serves to characterize the rest of his critique of the party system and representative government as a simple tendency towards authoritarianism. He liked government, or 'men', to take a firm hand, and he disliked opposition of any sort which might hinder this. Unqualified praise goes to Shepstone, for instance, who, reliable historians maintain, ruled so autocratically in the Transvaal as to have been one of the causes of the Boer rebellion.[5] Exactly what sort of government Haggard would have preferred is unclear, even to him. His obvious relish for the no-nonsense government of 'men' was somewhat moderated by its resemblance to what he saw as Boer anarchy. His fondness for the stability of British law was reduced by its oppressive bureaucracy. But with all his doubts, Haggard never questioned the wisdom of the imperial movement and retained an unshaken belief in England's historical role.

This general analysis of the politics of Haggard's romances has focused specifically on his views of militarism, Radicalism, commercialism, and the party system. These views, which comprise a large part of his propagandizing, are clearly consonant with the state of crisis in Great Britain during the imperial age. In distilled form, they become a transparent indictment of English life, perhaps strangely condemnatory coming from an imperialist, but understandable in view of the fact that imperialism itself was seen as an agent of moral regeneration. This latter function of imperialism prompts a consideration of Haggard's views on questions of heroism, spiritualism, and race, which will be presented in the remaining chapters.

Chapter 3

SOME TALK OF ALEXANDER: THE IMPERIAL HERO

However debased the reality of imperial heroism, the myth of the noble British soldier doing his duty for King and Country had enough currency in the early twentieth century for the singularly unheroic experience of the First World War to come as a severe blow. The work of the soldier poets, Sassoon, Owen, and Isaac Rosenberg, did its best to destroy what Owen called 'The old Lie' in 'Dulce et decorum est', and this end of the hero, as he was known to imperial Britain at any rate, was marked by some telling death notices: *Parade's End* (Ford Madox Ford, 1929), *Death of a Hero* (Richard Aldington, 1929), and *Goodbye to All That* (Robert Graves, 1929). In its intensity, the post-war disenchantment with heroics was unquestionably a reaction to the bravado of the pre-war generation. Armed with a yet untarnished cause, the earlier generation – that of Haggard and his kind – had made sacrifice and service popular bywords in the rhetoric of Empire. Anglo–German tensions, along with unstable relations with Ireland, India, Egypt, and South Africa, had elicited sympathy for the idea of both the heroic man, such as Gordon, and an heroic society. Successful expansionism was reason itself to revere what seemed extraordinary acts of individual and collective courage.

Haggard, part of that earlier generation of imperialists whose legacy of heroic idealism would be shattered in the trenches of the western front, viewed the war as a manifest confirmation of English heroism. For Haggard, English heroism was ineradicable. Those soldiers who died in the early days of the war, he wrote in a letter to *The Times*, upheld an heroic tradition and, what is more, negated by their example invidious reports of English decadence:

Not only are they crowned with fame, but by the noble manner of their end they give the lie to Bernhardi and his school, who tell us that we English are an effete and worn-out people, befogged with mean ideals; lost in selfishness

58

and the lust of wealth and comfort. Moreover, the history of these deeds of theirs will surely be as a beacon to those destined to carry on the tradition of our race. (10 October 1914, p. 9)

Compared with the warning cry of *Queen Sheba's Ring*, this assertion of strength sounds a shade contradictory. But both voices were part of the imperial atmosphere, expressions of its paradoxical mixture of insecurity and aggression. If there is some inconsistency in Haggard's damning and praising, however, there is none in his lauding of heroism; the hero, be he an Orme or a Quatermain, is a constant and unvarying ideal.

Many romance heroes of the late nineteenth century, Haggard's included, often have no explicit links to Empire. Their connection is felt rather than intellectualized and depends on a fervid preoccupation with manhood and an insistent emphasis on the virtues of strength and valour. Malcolm Elwin, writing of the year 1887 in *Old Gods Falling*, said: 'Beards and moustaches were the fashion, because they were the emblem of man's physical superiority, and the heroes of fiction were ... hirsute he-men, bred in the Kingsley school of muscular Christianity, like ... Rider Haggard's Viking-like adventurers' (1939, p. 23). The initial stages of professional athleticism, the deification of the championship performer, and the beginning of modern spectator sports, all of which cover this same time period, entertain a similar spirit of heroism. John Hobson, who singled out the spectatorial aspect of English society as particularly characteristic of its jingoistic atmosphere, suggested that field heroes and war heroes, by providing vicarious experiences of action, fed a neurotic imagination (1901, p. 12). The heroes of literature, then, were the imaginary reflections of a society interested in soldiers, athletes, and sheer physical power.

The late nineteenth-century emphasis on heroics grew out of both earlier cultural traditions and an antagonism to modern civilization. Among the earlier influences, the most notable is the figure of Carlyle, whose 1840 London lectures (which later appeared as *On Heroes, Hero-worship, and the Hero in History*) exalted the ideas of great men and their leadership. His veneration of the hero, moreover, coalesces with his critiques of industrialism and democracy so that we can see more than one familiar strain of thought. Victorian poetry, too, doubtless exerted its own influence, exploring and speculating on the nature of the heroic in the works of such writers as Tennyson and Browning. Paradoxically, Darwin and the machine age also assisted the cause of heroism by precipitating a defensive reaction. Romance heroes denied our unexalted biological origins along with the numbing effects of factory whistles and pistons.

Conversely, Darwin and industrialization had just the opposite effect on the realist literature of the period. Weakness and ineffectuality suffuse Hardy's *Jude the Obscure* and *The Mayor of Casterbridge* and bourgeois ignobleness stamps Flaubert's Charles Bovary and Homais as well as George Gissing's Jasper Milvain. Bourgeois society could be many things, but it could not be courageous or gallant. Sheer material success was not the stuff of heroism. Another writer who offers an interesting and significant contrast is Conrad, whose works perhaps surpass all others of the period in their preoccupation with the indeterminate nature of heroism in the context of a changing political and social climate. Although, of course, Conrad and Haggard were incomparably different authors, Conrad was Haggard's exact contemporary and shared his interest in the romance of adventure. A writer whose concern with the psychology of his characters has led to his being considered a 'modern', Conrad seems to have felt that the heroic tradition was at an end, and he was concerned, chiefly in *Lord Jim* and *Heart of Darkness*, with the failures of conventional heroism.

One might say that the hero is in a state of crisis in Victorian fiction. Mario Praz notes this and points out that in poetry women, rather than men, come to dominate the scene, assuming the posture of the *femme fatale* (2nd edn 1970a; 2nd edn 1970b). But the spectre of the *femme fatale* was also common to imperial enthusiasts, Haggard's Ayesha being the apotheosis of the fatal woman. Imperialists were also tainted with misogyny. The portrayal of Kipling's Maisie, the self-absorbed painter in *The Light That Failed* (1890), bears traces of it, as do the descriptions of some women in his short stories. Housman's young men suffer endless torments at the hands of faithless lovers; and Henley poetizes: 'I gave my heart to a woman –/ I gave it her, branch and root./ She bruised, she wrung, she tortured,/ She cast it underfoot' (1926, p. 163). Much of this amounts to little more than an affected romantic pose, but in bringing together the ideas of sacrifice, love, and death, even the pose is in keeping with the ideas hallowed by fictional heroes of Empire.

In literature, there are many variations on the heroic type, each revealing the individual beliefs and desires of its creator along with the character and disposition of his or her society. Heroes may be soldiers, artists, outlaws, gangsters, pagans, Jews, Christians, revolutionaries, or imperialists. Such figures may not always defend but almost always they reflect a society's sensibility. Thus we may feel comfortable with the veneration of a hero in one historical moment, perhaps when it means freeing a people from magic, superstition or fear, and uneasy about it in others, when it means bondage and oppression. In literature there are two principal kinds of heroes: the hero as rebel, the antagonist of society who (even if self-deceived) feels genuinely at odds with the prevailing culture, and the hero as defender. This latter may be part of one community or a source of regeneration for another, either of which he defends by his actions. He also represents the dominant forces of his society, and for this reason is represented as a national or racial type.[1] The arch-rebel hero of the nineteenth century – the Byronic hero – may be seen by some as yet another literary antecedent of the imperial hero, the latter being an extension and vulgarization of the type. However, the heroism of Empire is, at best, only very distantly related to the early rebel. The imperial hero, whether a soldier, an adventurer, or simply an embodiment of 'manliness', has no ideological dispute with his society – although he may believe that his society is losing its integrity, getting soft, or somehow straying from its true course. He is a hero who embodies its moral and social norms and turns restive only when his society exhibits signs of weakness. In the following discussion he will be presented as a traditional man of action who expresses the politically conservative aspirations of his society.

The literary wing of imperialism subscribed without reservation to the heroic way of life. Perhaps the best known enunciation of heroism, Henley's strident and chest-pounding 'Invictus' is too often seen as a personal and idiosyncratic response to the poet's own suffering. Although the personal note is there, this defence of stoicism is none the less imbued with the imperial ethos. A more public imperial stance comes to light in *Lyra Heroica* (1892), a boys' book of verse which Henley selected and arranged. In it Henley announced in his preface that he aimed 'To set forth, as only art can, the beauty and the joy of living, the glory of battle and adventure, the nobility of devotion – to a cause, an ideal, a passion even – the dignity of resistance, [and] the sacred quality of patriotism' (1921a, p. vii). Among the poems anthologized are Lang's 'The White Pacha', which deals with the death of Gordon, Stevenson's 'Mother and Son', an entreaty to mothers not to cry about sons sent on noble missions, and Kipling's 'Ballad of East and West', in which the heroic posture momentarily subsumes questions of race. Henley also includes his own 'Pro Rege Nostro' and 'Invictus', giving the latter the public place he felt it deserved.

To some extent, Stevenson also used the imperial environment to gratify his own personal needs. A note of stoicism is struck in his 'Requiem', for example, another poem children once routinely memorized for the purposes of imbibing patriotic sentiment: 'Glad did I live and gladly die,/ And I laid me down with a will.' That this militant stoicism was highly coloured by personal inclination is corroborated by Lloyd Osbourne, who recalls his stepfather saying that, were it not for ill health, he would have entered the army (1924, p. 38). Stevenson's physical incapacities, it seems, led him to glamorize army life. The impression we get from his writing, at any rate, is that personal concerns inform and shape political issues rather than the other way round. None the less, his admiration of individual heroics and his lauding of national heroics were usually of a piece.

The early essays of *Virginibus Puerisque* (1881), along with *Treasure Island* (1883) and *Kidnapped* (1886), gave Stevenson the reputation of a robust optimist with a special enthusiasm for national honour. In 'The English Admirals' he waxes nostalgic about England's historic past: 'There is nowhere such a background for heroism as the noble, terrifying and picturesque conditions of some of our sea-fights' (Stevenson, 1911, pp. 124–5), and 'In this desperate and gleeful fighting, whether it is Grenville or Benbow, Hawke, or Nelson, who flies his colours in the ship, we see men brought to the test and giving proof of what we call heroic feeling' (1911, p. 32). Stevenson also has humorous and slightly fanciful figures of heroism in other essays: 'the man who should hold back from marriage is in the same case with him who runs away from battle' (1911, p. 25), and a child playing at soldiers is 'young heroism with a sword' (1911, p. 158). The overall effect of the essays is one of healthy and youthful vigour, a salubrious stimulant for a thriving and militant race.

If Stevenson's heroic sentiment is fairly abstract in the essays, it is more precise in his last, unfinished work, *Weir of Hermiston* (1896). Revealing an extraordinary fascination with the will, Stevenson presents a law-and-order judge named Adam Weir whose overbearing demands for obedience lead him into direct conflict with his son. The entire novel is an examination of power and energy as one character tyrannizes over or falls under the sway of another. Archie, who sees a doomed victim of his father's harsh judgement stripped 'of his last claim to manhood' (1910, p. 370) just prior to being executed, is himself later unmanned when his father exiles him from Edinburgh to the Scottish countryside. In an interview with his father, Archie is finally led to pledge total obedience: 'Archie was now dominated. Lord Hermiston was coarse and cruel; and yet the son was aware of a bloomless nobility, an ungracious abnegation of the man's self in the man's office' (1910, pp. 385–6). The father's nobility is made comprehensible during Archie's exile, when his character looms over the Scottish countryside and is magnified by the stories of clan heroes. He is clearly intended as a large, splendid, and complex, however despotic, figure of elemental heroism. By juxtaposing the Scottish Highlands with Edinburgh, Stevenson suggests that the primitive energies which inform heroism are being crippled by civilization; the Adam Weirs are thwarted heroes in the modern world. Although the nature of the will is never settled, every turning of Stevenson's path leads back to the obscure road of Highland legend where preternatural forces reappear in unaccountable ways, so that heroism, however unresolved an idea, has something to do with tradition, with men of the soil, and with race.

Lang's writing, which also refers to Empire only in a few specific instances, similarly helped to nurture an imperial spirit with generous doses of heroic rhetoric. Lang had no direct hand in Empire building himself, but he had what Roger Lancelyn Green calls a 'reverence . . . for noble deeds and heroic actions' (1946, p. 51), specific examples of which can be found in his poems on Gordon and Isandhlwana. In general, Lang's interest in heroism was an aesthetic one: he admired heroic form. In his very influential criticism, this admiration showed itself in an excessive emphasis on the idea of manliness. In *Essays in Little* (1891) and *Letters on Literature* (1892), he reserved praise for works described as heroic, Viking-like, masterly, stoical, or athletic. He had a special fondness for writing that rejoiced in the joy of battle. In fact, the expression of ideas of manliness appears to have become his touchstone for literary excellence. Stevenson's 'Ordered South' is commended for its 'gallant and cheery stoicism' (Lang, 1891, p. 27). The Bible, Shakespeare, and Homer are acclaimed for their qualities of 'Manliness, courage . . . and a brave attitude towards life and death' (1891, p. 84). Dumas is the 'heroic and indomitable master' (1891, p. 1). Heroism, to Lang, is the uncomplicated conduct of an activist, the invoking of traditional ideas of heroic chivalry, ideas which were far removed from the military realities of Empire but which persistently remained a part of the imperial mythology.

Lang's vocabulary, built upon the heroic metaphor, is often called upon to work its magic in the unlikeliest places. Dickens's genius is attributed, in part, to his 'intrepid loathing of wrong, his chivalrous desire to right it' (1891, p. 131). Goodness becomes manliness – Browning and Arnold are admired for 'a certain manliness of religious faith' (1892, p. 9). And whatever other virtues Keats may have had seem to be overshadowed by his being 'really manly' (1892, p. 47). The validity of Lang's arguments is consistently undermined by the absence of any frame of reference other than that of war and battle. Charles Kingsley is said to be a favourite of boys because they 'take pleasure in his love of strong men, gallant fights, [and] desperate encounters' (1891, p. 155). Lang describes approvingly Kingsley's 'brave, indomitable belief that his own country and his own cause were generally in the right, whatever the quarrel' (1891, p. 155). Finally, the sagas are applauded because they are 'tales of enterprise, of fighting by land and sea, fighting with men and beasts, with storms and ghosts and fiends' (1891, p. 142). Icelandic men, Lang says fondly, feared nothing and were 'the best of soldiers, laughing at death and torture, like the Zulus, who are a kind of black Vikings of Africa' (1891, p. 44). All this and more make it easy to acknowledge Lang's own contribution to the course of manliness and combat.

Military metaphors abound elsewhere in Housman's *A Shropshire Lad* (1896), the poet's simple homage to the adolescent male. Maudlin as well as morbid, the poems associate young heroism with lost love and death, urging a stoicism that borders very closely on nihilism. Thus in 'The Day of Battle': ' "Therefore, though the best is bad,/ Stand and do the best, my lad;/ Stand and fight and see your slain,/ And take the bullet in your brain" ' (Housman, 1923, p. 86). Housman, like Lang, is generally more concerned with an heroic posture than with actual political issues. But a commitment to Britain is implicit in the writings of both men; it is an assumed allegiance which is supported by their sympathies for the heroic attitude.

Unlike either Lang or Housman, Henry Newbolt attaches more overtly political significance to the image of the hero. Newbolt, who sympathized with the Liberal-Imperialists, was a member of the Coefficients, a group gathered together by the Webbs for the sake of co-ordinating imperial policy. In *Admirals All* (1897), the heroic element is provided by naval glory. The title poem, 'Admirals All', largely a litany of heroic naval names, is a hymn to 'the bold and free' (Newbolt, 1919, p. 20). 'The Song of the Guns' honours those who die in service to England. 'The Service', a poem which ennobles self-sacrifice, espouses the familiar idea of life as a battle:

> And is not life itself, if seen aright,
> A great emergency, an endless fight
> For all men's native land, and worth the price
> Of all men's service and their sacrifice?   (1919, p. 62)

Newbolt has heroic poems for all occasions: 'Messmates' is one for dropping a sailor 'down the side' (1919, p. 40). The dying soldier in 'The Grenadier's Goodbye' manages, just at the moment of death, to summon enough energy to cry 'Forward, Grenadiers!' (1919, p. 106). Public school strains are similarly heard in 'There's a breathless hush in the Close to-night' (the poem that Orwell loved to hate) and 'The Best School of All'. The fight, the fray, the immediate experience is what counts in these poems. Good behaviour is manly or heroic, brave and courageous, and it is supported by platitudes such as 'Life is no life to him that dares not die/ And death no death to him that dares to live' (1919, p. 92). Peddled in such stock phrases, the heroic idea becomes a vacuous form.

In the case of Kipling, heroism is more than a series of conventional gestures. But the concern with the form of heroism, independent of purpose or social context, is again paramount. The form, or proper conduct, of the hero presumes his significance; action is synonymous with meaning. Arduous and demanding work, properly and faithfully executed, satisfied all heroic imperatives. It is sufficient that Kim takes part in the Great Game and that Findlayson ('The Bridge Builders') does his best as an engineer in India. Kipling's formula for heroic success allowed a man to achieve heroic status simply by proper regard for duty, discipline, and work. Heroism could be achieved by very different sorts of men: a Tommy Atkins, a Findlayson, or even a Gunga Din. Within understood limits of rank, each man was a potential hero. An entire nation could thus be heroic, if hierarchical. Heroism, then, was stratified, like society itself, and some heroes inevitably wielded more power than others. Leadership, the bulwark against anarchism, became vital. 'Lead us again, O Man-cub', a wolf of the leaderless pack begs Mowgli in 'Tiger! Tiger!', 'for we be sick of this lawlessness, and we would be the Free People once more' (Kipling, 1897, p. 134).

The Empire, with its twin burdens of exile and hard work, was the proper breeding ground for heroes, and – particularly in tropical and sub-tropical areas – it nurtured martyrs. In India, heat and sickness, in addition to the imperial grind, were persistent trials to even the most tenacious and strong-willed. For Kipling, India tested a man's mettle: 'Hard her service, poor her payment – she in ancient, tattered raiment –/ India, the grim Stepmother of our kind' (1919, p. 30). This Stepmother nourished and trained only for survival, and not always successfully at that: Hummil must give his life in 'At the End of the Passage', as must Bobby Wicks in 'Only a Subaltern'. Against such great odds, action itself engenders heroism.

India, however, was not the Englishman's only trial; sometimes heroes were made of those who ran up against an uncooperative home government or some particularly obtuse politicians. Like Haggard, Kipling felt that the English at home often failed inexcusably to recognize and appreciate the arduous work of its imperial servants. The colonial-speaker of the poem 'Pagett, M.P.' remembers the officious Member of Parliament who called him a 'bloated Brahmin' and talked of his 'princely pay'. This same Pagett is persuaded to stay in India for the rainy season, during which his bluster is gradually eroded by heat, insects, dust-storms, and illness. Another M.P. (Liberal) becomes a target for criticism in 'At the End of the Passage' when his intimations of an easy, indulgent Anglo–Indian life reach the newspapers in India. Very much like a Haggard protagonist, Kipling's hero is pitted against either the party politician or government bureaucracy.

For Kipling, heroic action is always linked to Empire but is not always imperial in nature. Kim's action is heroic, but the action of the engineer Findlayson is so only indirectly, because of his job. A job done well was vital to Kipling, independent of its relation to Empire.

But by affirming a code of obedience, discipline, and work, he strengthened the imperial cause. Propaganda comes in various forms. Ordinary Englishmen caught in the imperial web may indeed face existential crises, and Empire may well become a metaphor for isolation and exile; but isolation and exile set the conditions for undeniably imperial heroes. They may be prosaic in their dutifulness and simplicity, but their cause has a scrupulous particularity.

Haggard's heroes, like Kipling's own, are not always actively involved in the work of Empire. Although some have either just returned from or are about to embark upon an imperial assignment, many others find themselves on African territory for some strange but usually accountable reason. In general, Haggard's Africa is a vaster place than Kipling's cramping, constrictive, and almost claustrophobic India, and the heroism it calls forth is of the fresh-air sort – a quick battle with stupendous odds and equally stupendous deaths as opposed to the daily drudgery, exhaustion, and *ennui* that afflict the Kipling hero. And whereas Kipling forces his hero to struggle with his natural surroundings, Haggard lets the physical immensity of Africa enlarge the man. Thus Haggard's heroes are a more exhilarating sort. They are relatively free adventurers, and, like revivified De la Molles, they are English gentlemen above all things.

Quatermain, Haggard's most famous heroic character, is a self-reliant man of many talents. A trader, a hunter of wild animals, a warrior, and, after he finds his fortune in *King Solomon's Mines*, a propertied country gentleman, Quatermain is clever but, like Haggard himself, immodestly modest and addicted to self-conscious and pedestrian metaphysical philosophizing. The same rambling about the great questions of 'Life, Death, and Eternity' recurs in any number of books in which he appears. Quatermain manages to turn up, for example, in some fictionalized versions of imperial history. He is on hand when Piet Retief and the Boers are slaughtered by the Zulu chief Dingane in 1838 just outside Dingane's kraal and again at the battle of Isandhlwana during the Zulu War. But he regards it all from the position of bluff and hardy individualist – which ensures his physical mobility – rather than that of imperial servant. Other heroic characters, particularly ex-squire Curtis and retired naval-officer Good, are Haggard's tributes to the traditions of land and sea.

Since Haggard attempts to depict heroism mainly through spectacular and isolated events rather than through any developmental process, he leans heavily on the method of using a variety of right-sounding heroic words in much the same way as do Lang and Newbolt. Harold Quaritch has a forehead like Julius Caesar and a manly looking chin; Quatermain is compared to Nelson; Curtis is reminiscent of an ancient Dane; and John Neil is uncommonly strong and savage. Haggard's dealing with men solely in physical externals has the effect of endowing whatever is deemed heroic with a kind of mindless, insensitive amorality. This is apparent in *The Witch's Head*, when he describes Ernest Kershaw at Isandhlwana during a battle in which the captain of his regiment dies at the hands of the Zulus:

> Ernest feels his great horse gather himself together and spring along beneath him; he hears the hum of astonishment rising from the dense black mass before them as it halts to receive the attack; he glances around, and sees the set faces and determined looks upon the features of his men, and his blood boils up with wild exhilaration, and for a while he tastes the fierce joy of war.
>
> Quicker still grows the pace; now he can see the white round the dark eyeballs of the Zulus.
>
> '*Crash!*' they are among them, trampling them down, hewing them down, thrusting, slashing, stabbing, and being stabbed. The air is alive with assegais, and echoes with the savage Zulu war-cries and with the shouts of the gallant troopers, fighting now as troopers have not often fought before. Presently, as in a dream, Ernest sees a huge Zulu seize Alston's horse by the bridle, jerk it on to its haunches, and raise his assegai. Then the boy Roger, who is by his father's side, makes a point with his sword and runs the Zulu through. He falls, but the next moment the lad is attacked by more, is assegaied, and falls fighting bravely. Then Alston pulls up, and, turning, shoots at the men who have killed his son. Two fall, another runs up, and with a shout drives a great spear right through Alston, so that it stands out a hand-breadth behind his back. On to the body of his son he, too, falls and dies. Next second the Zulu's head is cleft in twain down to the chin. That was Jeremy's stroke.
>
> All this time they are travelling on, leaving a broad red lane of dead and dying in their track. Presently it was done; they had passed right through the Impi; but out of sixty-four men they had lost their captain and twenty troopers. As they emerged Ernest noticed that his sword was dripping blood, and his sword-hand stained red. Yet he could not at the moment remember having killed anybody. (1887c, p. 220)[2]

We are struck immediately by the inability of the passage to call up any imaginative or forceful visual image. Even Alston's sensational death is insipid. The general picture is the stock one of raised spears and undistinguishable men fighting *en masse*. Ernest Kershaw senses everything abstractly – he hears the noise of battle, the humming and the noisy shouting, feels the sensation of his horse beneath him and his blood boiling with 'wild exhilaration', and tastes the joys of war. The pace of the scene is typically fast and without any measure of reflection. It is significant that Ernest is in a dream-like state, and this is made to explain why he fails to remember killing anyone. (Battle scenes which end in the hero's frenzied delirium recur *ad nauseam* in other works.) The trance, coming as it does in a central passage of the work, has the trappings of both literary and psychological artifice. Haggard can offer up a surfeit of gore without being forced to implicate Ernest himself in its savagery. At the same time, he manages to make the battle, seen through such detached eyes, more defensible. Ernest's dream-like state is also a handy excuse for not sketching the demanding individual response to battle. But what is most striking about Ernest's dreamy perceptions is that they derive not from shock or fear, but from elation. His dream is euphoric, and his experience of war, is albeit mindless, exhilarating.

The Haggard hero is seldom if ever a reflective man. His wisdom comes from experience, intuition, and sudden insight, not from the reasoning of an intelligent mind. Like romance itself, with its discontinuous, disengaged experience, the hero is liberated from the demands of logic and philosophy. A man such as Ernest Kershaw need not worry about the deliberative and time-absorbing preoccupation with systematic thought; he follows orders, does his duty, and believes in his imperial cause. Haggard's defence of the hero, then, is plainly subversive of rationalism.

It is easy to see how the argumentative sparring practices of democratic government would disturb a man who had little time for rational thought. But Haggard's opposition to democracy reflects not only his anti-rationalism, but his contempt for the fact that, in his view, democracy nurtured the middle class and the unheroic man in an unheroic vulgar society, the society of opportunists and cynics, of Radicals, merchants, and traders. The bourgeoisie represented a commercial ethos, and a degraded culture. According to Eric Bentley, who examined the phenomenon of heroism as a nineteenth-century reaction to democracy in *A Century of Hero-Worship*, 'The Heroic view . . . is that democracy is pusillanimous and ignoble; it levels and belittles . . .; its aim is destruction of authority, redistribution of material goods, and a petty happiness' (1957, p. 123).[3] The bourgeois is equated with the city, effete urbanity, greed, and selfishness; the hero with the soil, the countryside, and the magnanimity of noblesse oblige. Far from being representative of the hereditary aristocracy, however, those who vilified bourgeois society were often dissatisfied elements within the bourgeoisie itself, and their statements of contempt were the expressions of a new spiritual aristocracy.

We need only glance at a work like *Colonel Quaritch* to detect Haggard's dislike of democracy and its parvenu upstarts. Radicals, Free Traders, and industrial leaders alike were unheroic by definition. Businessmen, lawyers, and politicians, too, could be seen as men without honour who contributed to the further emasculation of England. The most telling expression of Haggard's anti-democratic tendency is found in his enunciation of Anglo-Saxon superiority. Never a thoroughgoing doctrine, it is rather an unquestioned assumption, especially in the African stories. More often than not a Haggard hero is, like Arkle in *Treasure of the Lake*, 'a perfect specimen of the finest stamp of the Anglo-Saxon race' (1926b, p. 160). For the black, Anglo-Saxon supremacy is reduced to the simple question of colour – whiteness is all. In *Child of Storm*, Mameema, Haggard's Zulu Helen, recognizes Quatermain as a definitively higher type of humanity. He is 'white', she explains, 'one of those who rule' (1952, p. 60). Bes, Quatermain's Ethiopian slave in *The Ancient Allan*, remarks of his English champion: 'he is not a god but only that kind of man who is called a hero' (1920, p. 246). Like his real-life counterpart in Empire, the fictional white man is automatically elevated to the status of ruler. Leadership as an inborn characteristic, another feature of Haggard's fictional heroism, also points to his aversion to popular democracy. A male protagonist may be described as 'a man born to tower over his fellow men' (1892b, p. 274) or a man 'born to lead and not to follow' (1892b, p. 161). Even Umslopogaas, remarking to Quatermain on the behaviour of a snooping servant, falls into line on this point: 'It is his gift and duty to spy, as it is mine to smite with the axe, and yours to lead, Macumazahn' (1921, p. 201).

Not an aristocrat by birth, Haggard favoured the idea of natural superiority. In fact, Haggard's liking for sagas may well have been a reflection of this attitude. He claimed an affection for what he called in *Eric Brighteyes*, Haggard's own saga, 'that republic of aristocrats'

(1891, p. vii), the Icelandic community, where individual superiority counted for everything and society put few controls on men who wished to express themselves in action. Rather than an hereditary aristocracy he preferred a spiritual one, in which men might be natural-born leaders. There is even some suggestion that Haggard was attracted to theories of eugenics and favoured a eugenic programme to improve the quality of society. Under the headline 'Mr Rider Haggard on Poverty', *The Times* reported a speech delivered by Haggard to the Church Army at Bungay concerning the expense to the Imperial Exchequer of 'degenerates', specifically imbeciles and epileptics: 'He wondered ... whether society in self-defence might not adopt measures which would put a stop to the multiplication of the unfit' (15 July 1911, p. 11). Once again Haggard addressed himself to a perceived problem of decadence in English society, offering remedies that reveal not only a keenly felt racial consciousness but traces of social Darwinism.

While viewing Haggard's hero as a manifestation of anti-egalitarian tendencies helps to establish an historical context for such a character, examining the highly coloured sentiments conveyed by heroic tradition surely reveals its ideological punch. Traditionally, the hero is a model, an example of what is best in its most fully realized state. The specifics of this standard of excellence are derived from particular historical epochs, but they never move far from the spheres of religion, militarism, and patriotism. Feudalism produces a preponderance of military and religious heroes whereas nationalism produces patriotic heroes with good military references. The relationship of the hero to the natural world – the land, its people, its institutions – and, if applicable, to the supernatural one determines the shape of the heroic form.

When he is portrayed most dramatically, the hero is an agent of redemption, someone who comes, often from elsewhere, to restore a symbolically barren land; hence his regenerative nature. From the regenerative act emerges the hero as deliverer, a role that not only accommodates itself to paganism, Judaism, Christianity, or Islam, but comes to confer a religious significance on what are fundamentally secular acts. That is, the richly associative connotations of religion can lend not only legitimacy but sanctity to the activities of Empire. The imperial hero may be portrayed as merely an eminently able servant of certain national, historical, or even religious, forces.

The coming of a stranger-hero to a plague-ridden or dead land may be translated, in imperial terms, as the coming of the white man to the land of the black. In Haggard's fiction, the Englishmen who arrive in Africa usually find themselves in the midst of a crisis (nations are under attack from other nations, evil curses are plaguing the land, corrupt leaders are being defied by honourable challengers, powerful gods are about to be destroyed). They then enter the situation, tip the scales, and win the day. The particular pattern of old gods dying and giving place to new recurs with a certain regularity. The old gods are generally the gods of superstition that have kept their followers in ignorance, and their passing away is tantamount to the passing away of old civilizations. The potential for genuinely admirable heroic action in these situations is great, as C. M. Bowra remarked in his essay on 'The meaning of a heroic age' (1957):

in many parts of the world a heroic outlook has played a decisive part in history and done much to liberate mankind from primitive prohibitions and deterrents. Its chief use has been to discredit superstition by proving that a man can do more by his own efforts than by pretensions to magic.

(1964, p. 47)

The struggle against priestcraft and superstition is one of the ways in which, according to Bowra, 'man has emerged from primaeval savagery' (1964, p. 47), but the actual liberating process is a violent one, signifying a sharp break with the past.

Bowra offers the Zulu king Shaka as an example of one of the 'pioneers of a heroic outlook [who] bring the forces of priestcraft under some control' (1964, p. 29). Shaka set a trap for his priests, exposing them to his tribe after they were snared. In Haggard's *Nada the Lily* (1892), which tells this story, Shaka is angered by the tremendous powers of the 'witch doctors', or diviners, in Zululand and plots to free himself of these rivals. He secretly smears blood on his doors, which is interpreted as an evil omen, and then orders his 'witch doctors' to 'smell out' the devil who bewitched him. A gigantic 'Ingomboco' or 'smelling out' takes place, and the diviners, under orders from Shaka, single out man after man until the king reveals his hand and has them killed. Temporarily at least, Zululand is set free: 'Well, they are dead', Shaka says, 'and the land breathes more freely' (1892a, p. 63). Heroism of this sort, ferocious as it is, at least checks the tyranny of superstition.

Haggard illustrates this sort of heroic battle against superstition in his two most popular works, *King Solomon's Mines* and *Allan Quatermain*. In *King Solomon's Mines*, the triumphant Ignosi is quick to repudiate the old witch Gagool following the downfall of her ally, the evil king Twala: 'Thy magic could not save Twala, old she-wolf', he says, 'and it cannot hurt us' (1955, p. 202). Ignosi promises his white friends, Quatermain, Curtis, and Good, that he will do away with the 'smelling out' of wizards and put no one to death without trial. Under Ignosi's leadership, Kukuana society will experience a liberating reprieve from the scourge of superstition.

The battle against magic is central to *Allan Quatermain*, where the powerful priests of the Zu Vendis, who control virtually all the learning and law of the land, are pitted against the sympathetic White Queen, Nyleptha. A plot to marry Nyleptha to a supporter of the priests is thwarted by the timely arrival of Quatermain, Curtis, Good, and Umslopogaas. Nyleptha refuses to marry anyone but Curtis, and her intransigency sparks a full-scale civil war in which the priests are defeated. It is particularly among the educated Zu Vendis that the influence and prestige of the priests begins to wane, thus presenting the possibility of an enlightened society to come. The Zu Vendis, a special white civilization in the heart of Africa, seem to be a more exemplary people than other Africans in Haggard's stories, but even the Kukuanas of *King Solomon's Mines* are more admirable than most. In both books, the heroic quality of the Africans, which succeeds in raising them far above their usual position in the romances of Empire, comes from their battle against the powers of magic.

Paradoxically, these same works, which appear to praise Africans for severing their ties with wizardry and oppressive religious power, show the Englishmen fostering superstition (in *King Solomon's Mines*) and promising the benefits of Christianity (in *Allan Quatermain*). A claim to have mystical power, for example, shields Quatermain and his companions from a confrontation with the potentially hostile Kukuanas. Quatermain tells Twala that he and his friends come from the stars and that their rifles, along with Good's eyeglass, half-shaven face and white legs, are all magical. This subterfuge continues as the Englishmen make use of an eclipse as a 'sign' of their magical powers to win the confidence of Ignosi and some local chiefs. Ignosi remains forever ignorant of the real nature of the eclipse and accepts it as part of the Englishmen's 'magic': 'had ye not been Englishmen', he says, 'I would not have believed it' (1955, p. 145). Ironically, in this same passage Curtis expresses his wish that Ignosi free his people from the menace of wizardry. In *Allan Quatermain*, the Englishmen simply succeed in replacing one religion with another. The end of the book makes clear that Curtis, the new King-Consort, will introduce Nyleptha and her people to Christianity. The Zu Vendis are freed from a religion which held them captive and provoked a civil war only to be led to another religion imposed from above by a foreign occupier. The introduction of this missionary spirit tends to vitiate the significance of the heroic victory over the priests.

In later years, when Haggard was rehashing earlier plots, he wrote another story about Quatermain's efforts to rid an African people of superstition, *Heu-Heu, or the Monster* (1924), a title which could not have been more carefully chosen to match the insipid plot. Quatermain is needed because only a white man can kill Heu-Heu, the spirit god of a legendary tyrant turned monster. Heu-Heu's priests control the minds of both the Walloo, the people Quatermain saves, and the Walloo's enemies, a half-human and savage people named the Heuheua. The plot revolves around the appointed sacrifice of Sabeela, the Walloo chief's daughter, to the satanic god. Quatermain immediately becomes the 'White Lord' who, for Sabeela, was 'brought hither that we, who are bewildered and foolish, may drink of the cup of his wisdom' (1924, p. 125). Quatermain himself explains that he was 'brought here to play the part of a modern Hercules and clean out this Augean stable of bloodshed and superstition' (1924, p. 95). Again he fights the priests with 'magic' – the fire of matches and pistols – and deceives his confidante and ally, the Lady Dramana, by claiming that he and his servant '*are* in fact great magicians with much more power than we seem to possess' (1924, p. 164). If, as Bowra suggests, the fight against superstition is indeed heroic, the fostering of superstition can hardly be anything more than its opposite.

Of the heroes directly identified with the cause of Empire, Ernest Kershaw and his friends in *The Witch's Head* (1887) and Rupert Ullershaw in *The Way of the Spirit* (1906) are the most exemplary. Pleasant and well-mannered English gentlemen, they are much the same as the protagonists of other romances only with more explicit imperial ties. As imperial servants, they demonstrate loyalty, obedience, discipline, and self-control. If necessary, they are prepared to sacrifice their lives for both their cause and its ideals.

In *The Witch's Head*, Ernest, Alston, and Jeremy, a trio similar to that of Orme, Higgs, and Sergeant Quick in *Queen Sheba's Ring*, find themselves in the Transvaal during the annexation and volunteer to assist the British government during this difficult period. Ernest, a bright young man and able soldier, is another one of those gifted souls who are born to lead. After Alston, the older man of experience, asks him to be second-in-command to a small corps of volunteers in the Zulu War, Haggard gives his own stamp of approval:

Mr Alston could not have chosen a better lieutenant. He was known to have pluck and dash, and to be ready-witted in emergency; but it was not only that which made him acceptable to the individuals whose continued existence would very possibly depend upon his courage and discretion. Indeed, it would be difficult to say what it was; but there are some men who are by nature born leaders of their fellows, and who inspire confidence magnetically. Ernest had this great gift.   (1887c, p. 201)

This gift of leadership notwithstanding, Ernest also bears a strong resemblance to the young Haggard himself. Like Haggard, Ernest is a man of Danish extraction, an excellent campfire cook, and a jilted lover who countered depression with a short spell of intense devotion to horses, women, and hunting. Even Ernest's brush with death during a political mission to see a hostile chief is based on one of Haggard's own experiences. Ernest manages to avoid an ambush set for his return trip by insisting on a different route in order to get a better view of a certain moonlit valley in much the same way that Haggard avoided an ambush following a visit to Sekhukhune's kraal with Melmoth Osborn and Major Marshall Clarke.

The motive for Ernest's impetuous decision to alter his route underlines a key characteristic of Haggard's heroes, that is, their love of the African countryside. Ernest's constant and unblunted interaction with nature not only teaches him to make the quick decisions required of a hero, but it shapes his character and develops his potential: 'The continual contact with Nature, in all her moods, and in her wildest shapes, was to a man of impressionable mind, like Ernest, an education in itself. His mind absorbed something of the greatness round him, and seemed to grow wider and deeper during those months of lonely travel' (1887c, p. 134). This description of the effect of nature on Ernest is of interest primarily for what it suggests about Haggard's affinity for the African landscape, an affinity quite aside from his approval of a certain form of rule. The attraction to the land bulks larger in importance than the actuality of British supremacy. Empire was associated for him not so much with British rule as with a good healthy place to be; sharpshooting the wildebeest was surely preferable to battling the Boer, if less important. Haggard, like Ernest Kershaw, plainly enjoyed the African life he discovered, the sport, the food, the after-dinner pipes, and the telling of tales. Sitting round a campfire and sleeping under the stars was thrilling and intimate. After describing the pleasant evenings which, for Ernest and Alston, follow a day's shooting, Haggard addresses the sorry victims of civilized England and urges them to join the hunt: 'And so, my reader, day adds itself to day, and each day will find you healthier, happier, and stronger than the last. No letters, no newspapers, no duns, and no babies. Oh, think of the joy of it, effete Caucasian, and go buy an ox-wagon and do likewise' (1887c, p. 127). Haggard would send the enervated, unhappy European to the heart of Empire not so much to administer its government, laws or institutions, but for the chance to suck at the roots of vitality.

Unlike the men who serve Empire by choice, Ernest arrives in South Africa quite by accident. After taking part in a duel of pistols in France, he manages to avoid the authorities by escaping to the Transvaal. Soon he is granted a royal pardon during amnesty proclamations which grant immunity to all fugitives of the law who have assumed respectable places in the Transvaal. Since it is made very clear that the duel was forced upon Ernest, his breach of law is never a serious issue. Indeed, the duel enhances his heroic stature by establishing his impeccable honour. The manner of Ernest's transfer to the Transvaal is hardly irrelevant. It suggests a kind of 'accidental' hero and reduces the strength of the idea of scheming Empire builders. The English imperialist becomes just another casualty of civilization.

The notion of Empire as an escape-valve is convincing, although not all escapes are as dramatic as Ernest Kershaw's. Ernest's friend Jeremy Jones, for example, prepares to emigrate early in the book to flee what he perceives as lifelong enslavement to a law practice. Cambridge-educated but scarcely an intellectual, Jeremy is chiefly a presence of physical power, 'just the chap to cut down big trees in

Vancouver's Island or brand bullocks' (1887c, p. 21). At the first hint that something may be wrong with Ernest, Jeremy leaves his wretched office and rushes off to find his friend. Apparently to the battle born ('[t]he great deep chest, the brawny arms, not very large but a mass of muscle, the short strong neck, the quick eye, and massive leg, all bespoke the strength of a young Hercules' [1887c, p. 140]), Jeremy becomes a selfless and loyal friend. His most outstanding feat, which Haggard titles 'A Homeric Combat', occurs on a market square in Pretoria where, far from any military battlefield, he fights Van Zyl, the Boer giant, for flogging his servant. The episode also furthers Haggard's argument that the Transvaal annexation was necessary in order to protect the native blacks from Boer brutality.

The third type of hero in *The Witch's Head* is the colonial, who, ostensibly because he is untainted by English civilization, remains a figure of purity and a transmitter of the ideals of an older England. Ernest meets Alston, a character deliberately fashioned after Melmoth Osborn (Haggard, 1926a, I, p. 172), during the latter's first visit to England, and '[f]rom his open way of talking, Ernest guessed that he was a colonial' (1887c, p. 78). Formerly in the Natal Government Service, he had turned to big-game hunting following the receipt of a substantial inheritance. Alston is Ernest's second in the fatal duel in France, and he helps Ernest to escape from Dieppe to South Africa. Until his death at the battle of Isandhlwana, he remains with Ernest as teacher and guide. The familiar pattern of ordinary-man-turned-hero is repeated: Alston is 'a middle-aged man, not possessed of any remarkable looks or advantages of person, nor in any way brilliant-minded. But . . . his neutral tints notwithstanding, he was the possessor of an almost striking individuality' (1887c, p. 78). The leader of Alston's Horse in the Zulu War, he is the commonplace raised to perfection.

What ennobles ordinary men like Ernest and Alston is their upright conduct and their devotion to certain ideals. Ernest is a paragon of dutifulness: 'Even if . . . I knew that I must be killed twenty times', he says before Isandhlwana, 'I should go; I cannot run away from my duty' (1887c, p. 207). On the battlefield, with Alston dead and the fight a clear loss, Ernest exhorts his men to feats of bravery as he takes charge: 'Now, men of Alston's Horse . . . we have done our best, let us die our hardest' (1887c, p. 221). As the most fully drawn example of this heroic type, Ernest comes to shed a harsh light on the nobility of imperial ideals. What is disturbing about his seemingly honourable discharge of duty at Isandhlwana is that it comes directly on the heels of an admission of doubt concerning the wisdom of the war. Ernest's doubts, which precede the battle, not only make no difference to his behaviour but make no difference to his conscious-ness. Once an imperial policy is set in motion, it goes unchallenged and unconsidered. The admission of doubt comes during a farewell dinner in Pretoria just before the march to Zululand:

without expressing any opinion on the justice or wisdom of . . . [the Zulu] war, of which, to speak the truth, he had grave doubts, he went on to show, in a few well-chosen weighty words, how vital were the interests involved in its successful conclusion, now that it once had been undertaken. (1887c, p. 209)

Considerations of probity and ethics are confused with loyalty, national honour, and practical necessity. In the speech which Ernest delivers to the soldiers in his command, he justifies the war exclusively on the basis of patriotism and duty. Preaching a doctrine of blind heroism, he tries to explain what it is that unites the English in time of war:

'It is that sense of patriotism which is a part and parcel of the English mind' (cheers), 'and which from generation to generation has been the root of England's greatness, and, so long as the British blood remains untainted, will from unborn generation to generation be the mainspring of the greatness that is yet to be of those wider Englands of which I hope this continent will become not the least.' (Loud cheers.)

'That . . . is the bond which unites us together; it is the sense of a common duty to perform, of a common danger to combat, of a common patriotism to vindicate. And for that reason, because of the patriotism and the duty, I feel sure that when the end of this campaign comes, whatever that end may be, no one, be he imperial officer, or newspaper correspondent, or Zulu foe, will be able to say that Alston's Horse shirked its work, or was mutinous, or proved a broken reed, piercing the side of those who leaned on it.' (Cheers.) 'I feel sure, too, that, though there may be a record of brave deeds, such as become brave men, there will be none of a comrade deserted in the time of need, or of failure in the time of emergency, however terrible that emergency may be.' (Cheers.) 'Ay, my brethren in arms,' and here Ernest's eyes flashed and his strong, clear voice went ringing down the hall, 'whom England has called, and who have not failed to answer to the call, I repeat, however terrible may be that emergency, even if it should involve the certainty of death – I speak thus because I feel I am addressing brave men, who do not fear to die, when death means duty, and life means dishonour – I know well that you will rise to it, and, falling shoulder to shoulder, will pass as heroes should on to the land of shades – on to that Valhalla of which no true heart should fear to set foot upon the threshold.' (1887c, p. 210)

Invoking time-proven national ideals can cover any number of doubts and queries.

Ernest's speech presents a heroism which is more vulgar than the 'White Lord' fantasies of the Allan Quatermain legend. Rhetorically manipulative and limiting, it affirms the ideals of duty and patriotism as intrinsic virtues which have no reference to anything outside themselves, namely the Zulu War. Ernest has so internalized the association of Empire with righteousness that he subdues his 'grave doubts' so that they are merely incidental. Only the spiritual headiness of imperial work is conveyed. The Empire becomes an unquestioned good, defying rational explanation. Hence, an abstract spirituality becomes another feature of Haggard's heroism.

Rupert Ullershaw, the imperial hero of *The Way of the Spirit*, is the nearest thing to pure spirituality Haggard achieves in a character. A soldier, Egyptologist, and big-game hunter, he is also a repentant sinner. After a youthful and tragic escapade with a married woman, Ullershaw has vowed to heed his mother's advice 'to live for work and not for pleasure' (Haggard, 1906, p. 19). His ideal is renunciation, 'the way of the Spirit' (1906, p. 20), and pursuit of this ideal leads him to a commission in the Imperial army, first in India, where he takes part in two frontier wars, and then in Egypt and the Sudan, where he is a member of the relief expedition sent to rescue Gordon. At the beginning of the book, Ullershaw is a lieutenant colonel in the Egyptian army with a spotless record and an absolute devotion to duty. He is the product of 'work, thought, struggle, and self-control' (1906, p. 21). His favourite hero is none other than Gordon, 'the man he had known, loved, and revered above all other men' (1906, p. 122). Simple and unassuming, he cares little about the title and fortune he is to inherit from Lord Devene: 'he had no liking for this kind of inherited pomp which he had done nothing to earn, or for the life that it would involve' (1906, p. 42). Ullershaw is yet another of those shining examples of the perfection of the ordinary.

A bona fide hero – he misses getting the Victoria Cross only because of certain bizarre award procedures – he underplays the importance of all he has done and is embarrassed when forced to listen to accounts of his bravery. This is not to say that many people aside from his family and a few members of the War Office are even aware of his achievements. Haggard implies throughout that Ullershaw is just one of those many unsung heroes of Empire who suffer the neglect of a thoughtless and indifferent society. He was appointed to an office on the Persian Gulf and, Haggard writes, 'although he never got the full public credit for it, was fortunate enough to avert a serious trouble that might have grown to large proportions and involved a naval demonstration' (1906, p. 22). When Ullershaw agrees to go on a dangerous mission to the Sudan, Lord Devene says of the men who take on such tasks: 'They pass away in a blaze of glory and become immortal, like Gordon, or they vanish silently, unnoted, and unremembered, like many another man almost as brave and great as he'(1906, p. 137). Like so many other professional soldiers, Haggard suggests, Ullershaw does his job without being properly recognized.

More direct if equally familiar indictments of English society are made by opposing Ullershaw's simple nobility with the sophisticated worldliness of Lord Devene. Ullershaw finds his dinner at Devene's almost unendurable: 'Most heartily did he wish himself back in the society of old Bakhita, or even of the Sheik of the Sweet Wells [his Arab captor], in the Soudan, or in any other desolate place, so long as it was far from Mayfair' (1906, p. 66). And later on, while recovering from wounds in a Sudanese oasis called Tama, his mission failed and his military future in doubt, the same comparison of Africa and England reappears:

> those palm and mountain-tops, those bubbling waters and green fields, that solemn, ruined temple and those towering pylons, were better than the parks and streets of London, or that hateful habitation in Grosvenor Square [Lord Devene's] ... Indeed, had it not been for Edith [his wife] and his mother, Rupert would, he felt, be content, now that his career had gone, to renounce the world and live in Tama all his days. (1906, p. 206)

Ullershaw does renounce 'the world' to live in Tama; and Haggard justifies this renunciation, which involves the termination of active work in Empire, by destroying his character's career. The mutilations he suffers at the hands of some hostile Arabs who torture him – they 'hacked off his right foot ... burnt out his left eye and scorched his cheek with a hot iron' (1906, p.182) – disqualify him from future soldiering. (They also cause his wife to reject him.) And his failed mission, which in England is interpreted as a bungled mission, along with his discredited name, renders him unfit for any kind of Empire-related civilian work. After rejecting suicide, Ullershaw decides to live in Tama and, about halfway through the book, turns from imperial soldier to eastern saint.

However awkward the transition, it is related structurally and thematically to Ullershaw's sense of idealism. In the imperial section, his ideal of renunciation is expressed in terms of his duty to Empire. His personal concerns are set aside for public ones because 'the watchword of life should be Duty and Self-effacement for the common good, the greatest gain of man' (1906, pp. 78–9). When asked to go on a mission to the Sudan on the very day of his marriage, he hesitates, but when the Secretary of State reminds him that he is 'a man who sets duty above every other earthly consideration' (1906, p. 128), Ullershaw agrees. 'You used the word duty, sir', he says, 'and therefore I have little choice in the matter' (1906, p. 129). Renunciation also figures in Ullershaw's brush with death in the Sudan. He is offered a choice of 'death or Islam' by his Arab captors and, rather than swear allegiance to Islam, naturally chooses death, maintaining that, 'You can bind my body, but not my spirit' (1906, p. 181). After being tortured and mutilated, however, he is saved by the soldiers of Tama whose leader, Mea, is thereafter Ullershaw's spiritual mate.

In the second half of the book, Ullershaw, having found Mea, renounces sexual love. Although married to an unsuitable and unloving wife, he insists upon keeping to the letter of his marriage bond. The renunciation of sexual love, however, is only the most dramatic example of Ullershaw's asceticism. He also abstains from alcohol and tobacco, lives austerely, gives charity to the poor, doctors the sick, and dispenses justice. He is known throughout Tama as Zahed, the Renouncer, a public as well as a private saint. But strip away the pious and humble cover and the familiar 'White Lord' is apparent. Whatever the variation, Haggard's heroes are always reducible to this basic type. It comes as no surprise to learn that Rupert has helped turn the land of Tama into 'an Eden flowing with milk and honey' (1906, p. 292) or that he has made the oasis impregnable through his military knowledge of fortifications. This emphasis on the land and the military is more familiar Haggard territory, but it is strategically close to his spirituality.

Ullershaw's situation is presented as a problem of whether or not a western man who finds himself in the east is bound to western law, specifically to the marriage contract. As Haggard puts the question, 'should or should not circumstances be allowed to alter moral cases?' (1906, p. 10). The answer seems to be that, intentions and consequences aside, absolute and not relative moral principles must prevail. In no other work has Haggard delineated his philosophically idealist world view so revealingly as in this one. Ullershaw and Mea are prepared to forgo all hope of consummating their love for the sake of a bond to a woman who cares nothing for her lawful husband. When he comes into the Devene fortune and his wife seeks him out, he must decide either to remain with Mea, the woman he loves, or to return to his wife, the woman he despises. Although western law triumphs, the wisdom of Ullershaw's decision to return to his wife can never be determined by examining its results since Haggard avoids any judgement by having his hero contract and die from nothing less than bubonic plague! Abstract ideals, he ends by saying, are to be faithfully adhered to as a basis of morality, regardless of the cause or consequences of the actions taken in their name.

For Haggard, then, heroism is the spiritualizing of the temporal world, the investing of a special piety and sanctity in wholly secular acts by associating these acts with a fidelity to ideals, those, for example, of duty, obedience, and work. Such heroism finds its logical place in the romance, a kind of fiction which, according to our analysis, is fundamentally idealist in character, presenting experience as a confirmation of *a priori* truths. That such heroism is wanting, chiefly because of its indifference to the realities of experience but also because of its indifference to the contingencies of cause or consequence (recall the liberated or disengaged experience as the central feature of romance) has been suggested throughout this chapter. If there is any genuine heroism to be found in Haggard it exists in the Zulu story *Nada the Lily* and perhaps in the Zulu trilogy, *Child of Storm, Marie*, and *Finished*. The focus on Zulu history and life gives the readers of these works a sense of depth that they do not get from the stories that concentrate on English adventurers. Cut off from their roots, Haggard's English protagonists scarcely get wet in the shallow waters of their rough and tumble lives. Curiously, it is precisely this severance from home which, for Haggard, enables the Englishman to understand what it means to be English. Articulating what his fiction makes clear, Haggard claims in a letter to *The Times* that 'the Englishman is by blood and taste a trader, a traveller, a fighting man; all, indeed, that goes to make what is known as an adventurer' (1 May 1923, p. 15). He needs Africa, India, or some distant Ruritania to act out the role of his destiny. Haggard does not see that the distance he puts between his heroes and England is much more than geographical and militates against their heroism. Their relationships between both their home and their host societies are incomplete and unsatisfactory. The questions that remain unanswered – questions that help to clarify these incomplete and unsatisfactory relationships – involve the co-ordination of individual and collective will.

Chapter 4

AN INTELLIGIBLE ORDER:
HAGGARD'S FATALISM

If the British Empire is to fill its true place in the world it must first find its true place in the heart of its own subjects: they must have a reason for the national faith that is in them. That reason will be given by the analysis of the laws of British power and of the conditions which justify its exercise. This final inquiry will set out not from the assumption that might is right, which is the creed of despotism and the argument of caprice, nor from the theory that right is might, which is the mistake of shallow enthusiasts, but from the conviction that the universe is the manifestation of an intelligible order inseparable from the order revealed in the process of thought; that the laws of the material and of the moral world arise from the same sources, and are but different aspects of the same reality.   (Spencer Wilkinson, *The Nation's Awakening*, 1897)

Stevenson's image of the world as 'a brave gymnasium'[1] is a fair approximation of the blend of affirmation and activism that characterized the mood of romance in the late nineteenth century. Appearing to strike a nice balance between sober discipline and enthusiasm, it is usually this image that is assumed in the claim that romance, whether in fiction, verse, or temperament, was a reaction to a general malaise of lassitude and literary effeteness in particular. In his study of Henley, Jerome Hamilton Buckley begins with a discussion of the 'counter-decadence' of 'Invictus', arguing that, 'Essentially, "*Invictus*" was an inversion of Victorian defeatism into terms of personal assent. It proclaimed the militant optimist, the soul unconquerable whatever gods might be, the rebel strong in his revolt against death and denial' (1945, p. 26). To equate the spirit of romance with a healthy and virile optimism, however, is inaccurate. Although instinctively antipathetic to pessimism, the romance enthusiasts were not, after all, immune to the seemingly endemic malady of doubt that so affected the period. They merely chose not to be disabled by it. While pessimism was rejected out of hand, stoicism and its near relative, fatalism, were heartily endorsed.

84

In the world of Empire, the stoic does what is most important to do under circumstances of uncertainty: he acts. Citing Kipling's poetry as an example of this stoical activism, David Daiches adduces 'Recessional' as an illustration of the uncertainty that prompts a cautionary tone and a spur to careful action. For Kipling, Daiches writes, 'imperial dominion will be self-defeating in the end, yet one must go on paying a terrible price for it' (1969, p. 23). Thus, in Kipling's 'The Young British Soldier':

> If your officer's dead and the sergeants look white,
> Remember it's ruin to run from a fight:
> So take open order, lie down, and sit tight,
>   And wait for support like a soldier.
>   Wait, wait, wait like a soldier...
> When you're wounded and left on Afghanistan's plains,
> And the women come out to cut up what remains,
> Just roll to your rifle and blow out your brains
>   An' go to your Gawd like a soldier.
>   Go, go, go like a soldier...
>   So-oldier *of* the Queen.   (1919, p. 476)

Here is the world again as a brave, if grimly exacting, gymnasium.

While stoicism features significantly in romance literature, it is primarily an attitude to experience and carries no implications of faith in any cosmological order. It can be the philosophy of both the faithless and the believer. In Haggard's writings, stoicism is tempered alternately by faith in a divine order and an anxious scepticism. On balance, however, his writings are fatalistic and express faith in the existence of some universal design. The most obvious connection between fatalism and imperialism involves an understanding of Empire as either divinely or humanly willed. Does the source of the imperial hero's power come from within or without? Is it derived from the material or the supernatural world? For Haggard, these questions posed a problem that pervades his works. He even wondered how far the role of financiers, government, or the military, that is, the objective conditions of Empire, was causative. Human power seemed indeterminate and indeterminable.

While the conflicting theories of free will and determinism are beyond the limits of this discussion, some basic questions may be raised: How much power do we have if all – or nothing – is determined? Is it possible to reconcile free will with coercive external forces? How are the desires of the individual will brought into harmony with the desires of the collective will? Are the hero's individual acts good for the collectivity? As an instrument of God or fate, the individual will merges with that of the collectivity. Without the sanctifying supernatural element, of course, individual action becomes rather more questionable.

It would be wrong to claim that Haggard's notion of heroism, even granting its suggestions of innate leadership and racial and class superiority, presents a strict parallel to either a Nietzschean idea of pure will or the Social Darwinist idea of the survival of the fittest. Haggard's adventurer, the traditionally solitary man, is explicitly linked to a group, and his devotion to Empire often involves a submergence of self. But Haggard advances a curious variation of both the Nietzschean and Social Darwinist theories by replacing them with a rather crude concept of fate. The Haggard hero is not so much born to lead as born to follow and answer the call of his destiny. If a man's destiny happens to demand that he lead others, then so be it. The Englishman's destiny had called him to build the Empire, and the proof of this destiny was in the fact of Empire itself. By a roundabout route we return to Nietzsche and Social Darwinism and, along the way, seem to have placed moral responsibility at the door of that mysterious force of Fate.

The hero, then, is not as central to Haggard's fiction as is his fatalistic philosophy. Haggard simply could not accept the idea of chance and the chaos he felt went with it. He preferred a spiritual determinism, or fatalism, which offered the security of a supernatural force even though it seemed to erode, if not deny, consciousness, creativity, and moral responsibility. Whatever role is played by the factors of the material world, it is superseded by this spiritual determinism, the indefinable nature of which opens the door to a hazardous irrationality and a belief in the necessity of what is. This defence of the status quo by faulting the exigencies of God or Fate is not far from the notion of the survival of the fittest.

If there is any unifying element in Haggard's writings, it is his fatalism. Admittedly the most tedious aspect of Haggard's writings, it is also the most vital. In *The Days of My Life*, passage after passage underscores the fatalistic turn of mind brought to bear on Haggard's daily affairs. Early in the autobiography Haggard comments on his abortive attempt to enter parliament and his eventual abandonment of the career of statesman in the following way:

Fate has shut those doors in my face. The truth is that 'man knoweth not his own way': he must go where his destiny leads him. Either so or he is afloat upon an ocean of chance, driven hither and thither by its waves, till at length his frail bark is overset or sinks worn out. This however, I do not believe.

(1926a, I, p. xxi)

Haggard's faith in an ultimate and pre-existent order is repeated with regularity, and passages like the following can sound all too easily at times like his fictional characters:

Years ago I came to the conclusion that our individual lives are not the petty things they seem to be, but rather a part of some great scheme whereof we know neither the beginning nor the end. The threads of our destinies, in black or in scarlet or in sombre gray, appear and disappear before our mortal eyes, but who can figure out the tapestry that they help to weave?

(1926a, I, p. 100)

At times his fatalism becomes more conventionally religious and fate becomes equivalent to God. Then the need that Haggard had for such a faith becomes clearer, as does the relationship between religious conviction and secular anxiety: 'I hold that God and a belief in a future life where there is no more pain and tears are wiped from off all faces are necessities to civilised and thoughtful man, and that without them, slowly perhaps, but surely, he will cease to be' (1926a, II, p. 45).

Haggard's fatalism is a form of religious eclecticism. Although he sometimes expresses a traditional Christian point of view, he is just as likely to espouse an unorthodox one encountered in his varied readings. At times he seems as open to Buddhism or Islam as to Christianity, and the very fluidity of his ideas makes his fatalism difficult to define with any precision. As Morton Cohen says, Haggard

is not content with the answer of 'God' . . . His gropings into Egyptian and Nordic archeology, his scrapings in prehistoric temples and tombs, his toying with spiritualism and psychic phenomena, his strong belief in reincarnation – all are part of his quest for the answers. (1968, p. 224)

Whatever shape this quest takes, it always expresses Haggard's need for an ulterior frame of reference, a rationale for life.

Haggard's fiction dramatizes the antipathetic connection between design and chance through the conflict between morally virtuous characters who believe in universal order and morally suspect characters who have faith in chance alone. He ordinarily tries to condition the reader's regard for his characters through their belief or disbelief in a divine order. In the case of Alston, the sceptical colonial in *The Witch's Head*, Haggard's sympathy reflects an unusual attempt on his part to present virtue in the dress of uncertainty. Alston's character is based on Melmoth Osborn, the British Resident in Zululand in 1880 who supervised the activities of thirteen Zulu chiefs. Haggard remembers Osborn affectionately in his autobiography, but states that he 'never quite fathomed his religious views' (1926a, I, p. 172). One night Osborn apparently gathered a handful of ants and asked Haggard what difference there was between these creatures and themselves. Such scepticism was clearly disturbing to the young Haggard and so impressed him that he retained it in his later portrayal of the man. Whatever sort of glimpse Osborn allowed Haggard of his religious views, it clearly stayed with him as a kind of spiritual legacy which he proceeds to explore in *The Witch's Head*, his first story with an African setting.

Alston tells Ernest that the latter's belief that 'we shall live many lives, and that some of them will be [lived in heaven]' (1887c, p. 213) is presumptuous. He captures a number of flying-ants in his hand and demands to know how they are different from people:

'Just think how small must be the difference between these ants and us in the eyes of a Power who can produce both. The same breath of life animates both. These have their homes, their government, their drones and workers. They enslave and annex, lay up riches, and, to bring the argument to an appropriate conclusion, make peace and war. What, then, is the difference? We are bigger, walk on two legs, have a larger capacity for suffering, and – we believe, a soul. Is it so great that we should suppose that for us is reserved a heaven, or all the glorious worlds which people space, for these, annihilation? Perhaps we are at the top of the tree of development, and for them may be the future.'

Not only is he far less certain of an immortality such as Ernest envisages, but his own perception of the world is surprisingly harsh: enslavement, annexation, colonies, wars, and suffering. He plays devil's advocate to the younger, unworldly man, perhaps duplicating Osborn's behaviour with Haggard.

When Ernest asks him about his religious views, Alston responds with a Haggardian eclecticism:

'Religion? Which religion? There are so many. Our Christian God, Buddha, Mohammed, Brahma, all number their countless millions of worshippers. Each promises a different thing, each commands the equally intense belief of his worshippers, for with them all blind faith is a condition precedent; and each appears to satisfy their spiritual aspirations. Can all of these be true religions?'   (1887c, p. 213)

Since this is an early work (1887) and Haggard's later religious views remain similar, if more optimistic, it seems likely that Haggard was affected by Obsorn, whose fictional counterpart vents the doubts and uncertainties about faith Haggard was either too timid or too fearful to express.

When Ernest suggests that the same spirit underlies all religions, Alston concedes the possibility. He does in fact believe in God, but he rejects out of hand the notion of an eternity of either heaven or hell, and he categorically denies God's power to do evil:

'I do not deny the Almighty Power. I only deny the cruelty that is attributed to Him. It may be that from the accumulated mass of the wrong and bloodshed and agony of this hard world that Power is building up some high purpose. . . Our tears and blood and agony may produce some solid end that now we cannot guess; their volume, which cannot be wasted, for nothing is wasted, may be building up one of the rocks of God's far-off purpose. But that we should be tortured *here* for a time in order that we may be indefinitely tortured *there*,' and he pointed to the stars, 'that I will never believe.'
                                                                      (1887c, p. 214)

Alston's position does not amount to a denial of God, but to a refusal to associate God with punishment and retribution. His position is unorthodox, but so is Haggard's. Uncertainty plagues Alston, the chance that all the misery of life, in which he includes the misery of Empire, may be for nothing.

The effect of this conversation on Ernest is marginal. He is unshaken in his faith and the book concludes with a reaffirmation of his earlier belief in a paradise to come. The emphasis that the passage has in the book, however, and the way it accords in both tone and substance with some of Haggard's own religious unorthodoxy suggests that Haggard was more open to iconoclastic religious views than he allowed Ernest Kershaw to be. But if Haggard's mind could support religious eclecticism, it could not support spiritual chaos, and although he took little excursions over the border into scepticism, Haggard always returned to declare his faith in universal order.

Alston's final advice to Ernest, given by way of example, enjoins a stoical activism. He describes the code that he himself has lived by:

'I made three resolutions: always to try and do my duty, never to turn my back on a poor man or a friend in trouble, and, if possible, not to make love to my neighbour's wife. These resolutions I have often broken more or less either in the spirit or the letter, but in the main I have stuck to them, and I can put my hand upon my heart to-night and say, "I have done my best!" And so I go my path, turning neither to the right nor to the left, and when Fate finds me, I shall meet him fearing nothing.' (1887c, pp. 214–15)

The question of what determines our acts and of what purpose they are, Alston suggests, should not undermine action itself. Control over these forces matters less than one's daily moral struggles. Thus for Alston, fatalism invades the vacuum left by religious authority.

Ultimately, Haggard's heroes all seem to be controlled by fate. Like Haggard, they are 'philosophical' and express their views unhesitatingly. Quatermain, for example, who declares his fatalism in a number of tales, asserts in *Finished* (1917):

'I am a fatalist, one who knows full well that when God wants me He will take me; that is if He can want such a poor, erring creature. Nothing that I did or left undone could postpone or hasten His summons for a moment, though of course I knew it to be my duty to fight against death and to avoid it for as long as I might, because that I should do so was a portion of His plan.'
(Haggard, 1962, pp. 115–16)

Here we see Quatermain's fatalistic convictions, and the relationship of those convictions to duty and the working out of the universal pattern.

A similar belief in fatalism is declared in the much earlier *King Solomon's Mines* when Quatermain explains his decision to make the dangerous trip to Kukuanaland:

I am a fatalist, and believe that my time is appointed to come without reference to my own movements and will, and that if I am to go to Suliman's Mountains to be killed, I shall go there and shall be killed. God Almighty, no doubt, knows His mind about me, so I need not trouble on that point.
(1955, p. 46)

In *She and Allan* (1921), a story which brings Quatermain and Umslopogaas together with Ayesha and sets them against a sensational background of kidnapping, murder, cannibalism, and alcohol, Quatermain's view of a series of calamities is similarly fatalistic:

at times I think that these seeming accidents must be arranged by an Intelligence superior to our own, to fulfil through us purposes of which we know nothing, and frequently, be it admitted, of a nature sufficiently obscure. Of course this is a fatalistic doctrine, but then, as I have said before, within certain limits I am a fatalist.   (1921, p. 114)

Although fate in Haggard's fiction is usually brought into line with the idea of a benevolent God, as in the passage from *King Solomon's Mines*, it is occasionally stripped of its divine benignity and seen more starkly as a great indifferent equalizer. In *Allan Quatermain*, for example, Quatermain's geniality disappears as he equates fate with death: 'The great wheel of Fate rolls on like a Juggernaut, and crushes us all in turn, some soon, some late – it does not matter when, in the end it crushes us all' (1919a, p. 9). The cruel and persistent director of death, however, is also the creator of a purposeful world; unhappily, the prescience allowed to fate is not allowed to its victims, who must remain ignorant of their place in the grand scheme of things and whose ignorance sustains their belief.

By positing a transcendental force, or intelligence, moving behind the scenes, Haggard presents all acts, political as well as personal, as manifestations of some greater purpose. The rationalization that emerges is convenient because the belief that human acts and their consequences are directed from on high and have a significance we cannot presume to divine encourages imperial servants to submit happily to a greater force than their own and to cultivate a zest for obedience. Evolutionary theory went far to extinguish the lights of such belief, but it did not destroy faith altogether. Even Haggard himself, although not a supporter of evolutionary theory in any profound sense, inhaled the odd whiff of Darwinism and its diverse interpretations from the atmosphere. His most conscious efforts, however, went to support the teleological premises of his devotion to the cause of Empire.

Haggard's fictional expression of this belief in some grand design is particularly evident in *The Way of the Spirit*, a book which brings together philosophy and politics. Ullershaw's political involvement follows his religious, or spiritual, conversion early in a story in which politics and religion remain intimately connected throughout.

Thoroughly committed to an ordered cosmology, Ullershaw believes that

he should not live uselessly, or endure death in vain, that no life, not even that of the ant which toiled ceaselessly at his side in the yellow sand, was devoid of purpose or barren of result; that chance and accident did not exist; that every riddle had its answer, and every pang its issue in some new birth; that of the cloth of thoughts and deeds which he wove now would be fashioned the garment that he must wear hereafter.   (1906, pp. 24–5)

He also believes that 'the future is the gift of God and not shaped by man' (1906, p. 29). In such a manner he divests humanity of much of its power, but this scarcely disturbs him since he has learned to live according to a code of duty and renunciation. Even when mutilated by his enemies he claims that 'it is God's will, and I must bear it' (1906, p. 243).

Ullershaw's foil is the atheistical Lord Devene, whose reasoning faithlessness has led him to nothing but despair:

[he] had broken through all beliefs and overthrown all conventions, yet the ghost of dead belief still haunted him, and convention still shackled his hands and feet. For he could find no other rocks whereon to rest or cling as he was borne forward by the universal tide.   (1906, p. 12)

This spiritual emptiness accounts for his comfortless existence and his eventual breakdown. The opposition of Ullershaw and Devene is carefully engineered to illustrate the futility of the latter's atheism. Devene, the contemptuous iconoclast, eventually commits suicide, leaving Ullershaw a letter which amounts to a testimony of his atheism. Devene is so world-weary that he admits to not knowing why, except for the demands of habit, sentiment, and nature, people trouble to perpetuate their species:

To me it appears to be nothing more than a part of the blind brutality of things which decrees the continuance, at any rate for a little while, of the highly nervous, overbred and unsatisfactory animal called Man. Well, soon or late he will die of his own sufferings, that increase daily as he advances in the scale of progressive degeneracy, which he dignifies by the name of civilisation.
(1906, p. 286)

Devene sounds like a bitter Alston, a case of doubt become disbelief, and although treated with some sympathy, his 'fate' is none the less sealed by his atheism. It is Ullershaw and his spiritual reflections that we are to endorse:

He had grasped the great fact still not understood by the vast majority of human beings, that the universe and their connection with it is a mighty mystery whereof nine hundred and ninety-nine parts out of a thousand are still veiled to men. These are apt to believe, as Lord Devene believed, that this thousandth part which they see bathed in the vivid, daily sunlight is all that there is to see. . . They look upon the point of rock showing above the ocean and forget that in its secret depths lies hid a mountain range, an island, a continent, a world, perhaps, whereof this topmost peak alone appears.

(1906, p. 288)

A more disturbing example of Haggard's fatalism is found in *Finished*, the third volume of the trilogy concerning the rise and fall of the House of Shaka, or the Zulu nation. In some ways the trilogy represents the best of Haggard, but in *Finished*, which accounts for the downfall of Cetshwayo and the submission of the Zulus to the English as if they were part of some African substream of Greek tragedy, Haggard's historical embroidering is crude and excessive. Although Haggard knew that his fictional version of the Zulu War and the Battle of Isandhlwana bordered on distortion, he was apparently unconcerned.[2] The downfall of the Zulus is brought about primarily by the unknown power that directs all and only secondarily by elements internal to the Zulus themselves, while the British play a relatively minor role as the mere instruments of fate. That he was writing about a nation in whose well-being he often claimed a sympathetic interest makes *Finished* especially distressing.

Haggard describes *Finished* as a narrative of 'the consummation of the vengeance of the wizard Zikali . . . upon the royal Zulu House of which Senzangacona was the founder and Cetewayo [sic] our enemy in the war of 1879, the last representative who ruled as a king' (1962, p. xi). The motive of vengeance is established from the start, with the conflict between the Zulus and the British taking a wholly subordinate position. Zikali, so the story goes, a powerful and terrifying wizard whose wives and children were first robbed and then murdered by Shaka, lives only to take vengeance on Cetshwayo. For this purpose he enlists the aid of Allan Quatermain, thereby assuring the downfall of the Zulus. The period is just before the Zulu War, and the important decision to go to war turns on a council meeting at which Cetshwayo and his advisers must decide one way or the other.

93

Cetshwayo leans towards conciliation, hardly what the bloodthirsty Zikali wants. So Zikali, himself merely the instrument of a divine force, stage-manages the appearance of a white goddess, the Inkosazana-y-Zulu, who gives the Zulus a sign to fight.

That the spirit is not a spirit at all, but a white woman and friend of Quatermain's, changes neither the nature of the decision made by the Zulus nor the sense of inevitability created by the proceedings. As Haggard notes in the introduction to the book,

In this story the actual and immediate cause of the declaration of war against the British power is represented as the appearance of the white goddess, or spirit of the Zulus, who is, or was, called Nomkubulwana or Inkosazana-y-Zulu, i.e., the Princess of Heaven. The exact circumstances which led to this decision are not now ascertainable, though it is known that there was much difference of opinion among the Zulu *Indunas* or great captains, and like the writer, many believe that King Cetewayo was personally averse to war against his old allies, the English. (1962, p. xi)

If many people, including Haggard himself, believed Cetshwayo averse to war, accounting for his change in this way is more than curious. The result is a story that not only presents the Zulu War as simply part of the unalterable historical order of things but also nurtures the myth of a dark Africa where all is a morass of blood and confusion. The accumulated effect of premonitions, prophecies, spirits and vengeance is such that the Zulu nation seems fated indeed.

After giving his characters a fatalistic philosophy, Haggard often fails to provide them with any reasons for their actions. They repeatedly appear to act either on intuition or because of strange and inexplicable forces. Decisions are made by yielding to overwhelming inner promptings. These appear to have little to do with conscious choice and may more accurately be described as thrusting, elemental, or primitive, the sort of thing that made Haggard an obvious choice for Jung's discussion of the anima. Eventually the question of power comes into play again, and the liberty of Haggard's characters to act as conscious beings is seen as seriously limited. While it may be in the best spirit of romance for a character to be more emotional than analytical, to be a medium for special forces, to be unpredictable, inscrutable, and mysterious, such characterization has little to commend itself on Haggard's imperial terrain.

Quatermain's yielding to momentary impulse in *She and Allan* occurs when he loses the spoor of a tribe he is tracking and suddenly decides to take a certain path which, coincidentally, turns out to be the right one: 'some instinct within seemed to impel me to steer for it, although I had all but made up my mind to go in a totally different direction many points more to the east' (1921, p. 101). Quatermain is usually cast as a temperamental sceptic whose constant bombardment by things unaccountable – objects, experiences, and feelings – persuades him to abandon doubt. Even his life of adventure is attributed to a mysterious guiding force:

Often in my life I have felt terrified, not being by nature one of those who rejoices in dangers and wild adventures for their own sake, which only the stupid do, but who has, on the contrary, been forced to undertake them by the pressure of circumstances, a kind of hydraulic force that no one can resist, and who, having undertaken, has been carried through them, triumphing over the shrinkings of his flesh by some secret reserve of nerve power. Almost am I tempted to call it spirit-power, something that lives beyond, and yet inspires our frail and fallible bodies. (1921, p. 111)

Something like this same spirit-power also accounts for a number of his fortuitous escapes from ostensibly inescapable situations.

Quite often, Quatermain has a sense of himself as a conductor, as it were, of spiritual current. In *Treasure of the Lake*, he describes himself as 'by no means the chief actor in this business. Indeed, I was never more than an agent, a kind of connecting wire between the parties concerned, an insignificant bridge over which their feet travelled to certain ends that I presume to have been appointed by Fate' (1926b, p. 7). Quatermain's friend Arkle, the protagonist of the story, has come to Africa in pursuit of a woman whose image appeared to him in a dream. When she is eventually found, she claims to have 'drawn' him to Africa: 'For know that, from of old, your destiny and mine have been intertwined, and so it must be till that end which is the real beginning' (1926b, p. 175). Such is the potency of spirit-power.

In *Finished*, another book with its share of strangely motivated actions, Maurice Anscombe makes plans for a hunting expedition some eighteen months in advance because, he explains, 'Something in me seems to say that we *shall* make this expedition and that it will have a very important effect upon my life' (1962, p. 25). Anscombe's behaviour is consistently eccentric throughout. He and Heda, the woman he is to marry, decide whether to travel to Pretoria or Zululand by counting the seconds between lightning flashes. 'They just acted on intuition . . .', Quatermain remarks, 'namely a desire to consult the ruling fates by omens or symbols' (1962, p. 117). Such methods of decision-making in Haggard are always for the best, so the eventual good fortune of Anscombe and Heda comes as no surprise.

In addition to the oddly motivated characters of the Quatermain books, there is Rupert Ullershaw of *The Way of the Spirit*, who, yielding to an impulse to follow two potentially dangerous strangers into a desert temple, finds Mea, his soul-mate. She explains her own uncanny reasons for being in the desert with her entourage: 'have I not felt you [Rupert] drawing near to me, and therefore taken these people from their gardens and sat here for three whole days?' (1906, p. 254). Since Ullershaw has just arrived from England with no warning, Mea's intuition is wonderful indeed. In *The Ghost Kings* this same intuitive action is found in Rachel Dove, who claims that 'Something tells me what to do and say' (1908, p. 97). Richard Derrien, who saves Rachel from danger at one stage of the book, states, 'I don't know why I came. I suppose something sent me to save you' (1908, p. 13). And when this well-matched pair meet and embrace after a long period of separation, Haggard describes their kiss as 'the declaration of an existent unity which circumstances did not create, nor their will control' (1908, p. 126). Similar examples abound in this and other works.

Only once does Haggard state explicitly that the choice between instinct (or intuition) and reason is one which is governed by the African locale. When Leonard Outram acts on a prophecy in *The People of the Mist* (1894), Haggard observes that

he was no longer a civilised man; he had lived so long with nature and savages that he had come to be as nature makes the savage. His educated reason told him that this was folly, but his instinct – that faculty which had begun to take the place of educated reason with him – spoke in another voice. He had gone back in the scale of life, he had grown primitive; his mind was as the mind of a Norseman or of an Aztec.   (1894, p. 34)

Although many of the earlier quoted passages are from the works set in Africa and consequently imply that the yielding to instinct and impulse is a consequence of the landscape, virtually every one of Haggard's stories exhibits similar motives for action. This is not to say that the African environment does not appear to exert a special influence on Europeans which may be termed 'primitive', but that 'primitivism', for Haggard, was discovered within oneself. The struggle between instinct and reason occurs chiefly within the psyche. Geo-metaphorically, Europe represents reason and Africa intuition. In Africa, Haggard's European characters assume, people exist in natural harmony with their environment, this being the heart of primitivism. It is this assumed harmony that foreigners want to grasp, discovering not so much Africa as themselves.

Yet not all of Haggard's characters face life with the placidity of an Ullershaw. Temporary lapses of faith and expressions of outrage and despair are also a part of their fatalism. In *Colonel Quaritch*, in which Haggard's narrator says that 'This is not a very cheerful world at the best of times' (1888, p. 211), despair is manifested as a feeling of alienation: 'the greatest terror of our being lies in the utter loneliness, the unspeakable identity of every living soul' (p. 107). Such alienation is matched and overtaken by Hamarchis's anxiety and impotence in *Cleopatra* (1889): 'Alas! We shape our plans, and by slow degrees build up our house of Hope, never counting on the guests that time shall bring to lodge therein. For who can guard against – the Unforeseen?' (1889b, p. 136). Even a beneficent universe, it would seem, is often too difficult to accept.

Ignorance of life's purpose is still another source of misery and suffering. In *Treasure of the Lake*, it is Arkle, the West African adventurer, whose partial and deficient knowledge of himself leads him to say that 'here in the world we are but wanderers lost in a fog which shuts off glorious prospects, divine realities, so that we can see little except dank weeds hanging from the rocks by which we feel our way' (1926b, p. 163). And the narrator of *Beatrice* concludes the book on this very lowest of notes: 'Say – what are we? We are but arrows winged with fears and shot from darkness into darkness; we are blind leaders of the blind, aimless beaters of this wintry air; lost travellers by many stony paths ending in one end' (1892b, p. 312).

Significantly, such suffering is the natural mate of eminence and a check on the vanity that may corrupt the powerful. In the opinion of Jess, 'Suffering, mental suffering, is a prerogative of greatness' (1889a, p. 54). It is a test of worthiness – either one suffers and passes on to distinction or one is too plebeian to suffer and remains an undistinguished part of the crowd. Suffering becomes a measure of humanity, and relief from suffering consists chiefly in perceiving some spark of divine light. Regrettably, Haggard seems unable to conceive of suffering as having a distinct material origin. But readers who can may find his explanation of misery irritating in the extreme. Furthermore, many readers may not be able to banish the thought that whereas those who hold positions of authority can well afford to flirt with despair, others must pay the price of further dependence.

The sense of powerlessness that often accompanies Haggard's characters in their despair relates directly to the issue of free will and, by implication, moral responsibility. Free will means responsibility, and the lack of it must subvert responsibility and weaken the motive for action. If an action emanates from on high, then the ethical worth of what a person does becomes debatable.

Although Haggard concedes the importance of genetic, physical, and social factors in giving life shape (witness his exhortations to the English to breed more intelligently), he forgets them when he ventures an opinion on free will. He seems unable to say that the power to make choices is limited by circumstances and that someone can be, at the same time, both a producer and a product of causes. He wants to be able to say conclusively that free will either exists or does not. For the most part, he concludes that it does not, because we act out the designs of fate.

As the supposedly mature and worldly wise narrator of *Finished*, Quatermain considers free will a delusion:

The fact is, I suppose, that man who thinks himself a free agent, can scarcely be thus called, at any rate so far as immediate results are concerned. But that is a dangerous doctrine about which I will say no more, for I daresay that he is engaged in weaving a great life-pattern of which he only sees the tiniest piece.

(1962, p. 220)

What is 'dangerous doctrine' to Quatermain is 'perilous doctrine' to the narrator of *Jess*, who comments on Jess's sense of impotence when she sees John Neil in Pretoria after she has deliberately gone there to avoid him:

His sudden appearance was almost uncanny in the sharpness of its illustration of her impotence in the hands of Fate. She felt it then; all in an instant it seemed to be borne in upon her mind that she could not help herself, but was only the instrument in the hands of a superior power whose will she was fulfilling through the workings of her passion, and to whom her individual fate was a matter of little moment. It was inconclusive reasoning and perilous doctrine, but it must be allowed that circumstances gave it the color of truth.

(1889a, pp. 122–3)

As for the burden of responsibility or accountability which underlies the peril, Haggard gives some interesting, albeit inconclusive, consideration to the question in *The Way of the Spirit*. Edith Devene, who connives at attracting the husband she does not and cannot love, believes she ought to love him none the less. Her inability to love him, Haggard insists, cannot be helped: 'it was not her fault if she shrank from Rupert, whom she ought to, and theoretically did, adore. It was in her blood; for all her strength and will she was but a feather blown by the wind, and as yet she could find no weight to enable her to stand against that wind' (1906, p. 114). It is not simply a matter of Haggard's ineptitude in treating relationships between the sexes that makes him unable to say that Edith is not emotionally or physically interested in Rupert. His choice of words follows from his philosophy. He means to account for this lack of attraction on her part by attributing it to the blood, by making it both a matter of biological destiny and unchangeable spiritual incapacity.

Those of Haggard's characters who concede that there is such a thing as free will try to reconcile it with fatalism. Such is the case with Stella Fregelius who argues that free will fits in perfectly with her fatalism: ' "the material given us to weave with, that is Fate; the time which is allotted for the task, that is Fate again, but the pattern is our own" ' (1904, p. 157). But the 'pattern' is not much more than a rhetorical device. Form and content do not fall apart so easily in fact. In *Cleopatra*, Harmachis explains his own notion of the way free will and fatalism are reconciled: ' "we are free to act for good or evil, and yet methinks there is a Fate above our Fate, that, blowing from some strange shore, compels our little sails of purpose, set them as we will, and drives us to destruction" ' (1889b, p. 327). Quatermain makes another attempt to express the idea in *Treasure of the Lake*: 'Doubtless man has free will, but the path of circumstances upon which he is called to exercise it is but narrow' (1926b, p. 27). Ayesha recalls her father telling her, in *Wisdom's Daughter*, that 'without doubt my will was that of God' (1923, p. 24). And in still another work, *Colonel Quaritch*, Mrs Quest, about to retreat to a convent after a life of 'sin', proclaims that, ' "The mistake was mine; that is, it would have been mine were we free agents, which we are not" ' (1888, p. 273).

Haggard can make no firm decision on the issue of free will, but he clearly had a strong sense of not being free. Curiously, neither his personal nor his political success convinced him of his ability to shape his own destiny. His peculiar notions of causality very likely created this insecurity. It is not even that psychological or moral imperatives bind him, as they do others, with a felt sense of unfreedom. His 'causes' are, ultimately, unknown phantoms. (His failure to deal with the effect of character upon character is surely part of this inability to see the sum of human forces or wills that constitutes so much of causality.) He appears wilfully blind to the material causes of reality.

Unfortunately, Haggard's fatalism is a doctrine that ensures ignorance. It is thoroughly sustained by the belief that the purpose and meaning of life are inaccessible. This inaccessibility of knowledge fixes human bounds at once and places all meaning beyond the sphere of reason. Haggard's characters are, in the end, far more likely to trust their emotions than their intellect, making the romantic antipathy between emotion and intellect standard fare in the fiction.

Ludwig Horace Holly, the man who travels to central Africa and central Asia in pursuit of Ayesha and whatever she represents, is also a Cambridge scholar. So when Holly asserts that knowledge is forever hidden, his Cambridge background provides a suitably authoritative air. Speculating on the meaning of life, he laments the futility of the intellect:

the mind wearies easily when it strives to grapple with the Infinite, and to trace the footsteps of the Almighty as He strides from sphere to sphere, or deduce His purpose from His works. Such things are not for us to know. Knowledge is to the strong, and we are weak. Too much wisdom perchance would blind our imperfect sight, and too much strength would make us drunk and over-weight our feeble reason till it fell and we were drowned in the depths of our own vanity. (1957, pp. 128–9)

The exposure to Ayesha, whose wisdom is more than Holly can ever hope to apprehend, only serves to emphasize the relative ignorance of more ordinary mortals.

In another passage from *She*, Haggard suggests that such ignorance even blunts our perception of good and evil. Having horrified Holly with her plan to murder Ustane, a potential rival for Leo Vincey's affections, Ayesha tries to be reassuring:

'out of crimes come many good things, and out of good grows much evil. The cruel rage of the tyrant may prove a blessing to thousands who come after him, and the sweetheartedness of a holy man may make a nation slaves ... Good and evil, love and hate, night and day, sweet and bitter, man and woman, heaven above and the earth beneath – all these things are necessary, one to the other, and who knows the end of each? I tell thee that there is a hand of Fate that twines them up to bear the burden of its purpose, and all things are gathered in that great rope to which all things are needful.' (1957, p. 210)

That Haggard was quite aware of the conclusions to be drawn from Ayesha's speech is clear from Holly's response: 'I felt that it was hopeless to argue against casuistry of this nature, which, if carried to its logical conclusion, would absolutely destroy all morality, as we understand it' (1957, pp. 210–11). But Holly, himself a fatalist, adheres to a philosophy that is not very far removed from Ayesha's.

Thus fatalism, or *spiritual* determinism, is Haggard's equivalent of that scientific determinism known as Social Darwinism. Indeed, H. Stuart Hughes describes Social Darwinism as 'a kind of scientific fatalism' (1958, p. 39) in his *Consciousness and Society.* The similarity need not be pushed too far, but a few observable parallels are worth noting. First, there is the idea of natural, or rather supernatural, selection that pervades the entire philosophy.[3] Fate seems to know who it wants alive, dead, or acting out its divine decrees – the process is selective. It is implied in such statements as Geoffrey Bingham's, in *Beatrice*, that ' "In the long run . . . the world gives our due . . . If you are fit to rule, in time you will rule; if you [are] not, then be content and acknowledge your own incapacity" ' (Haggard, 1892b, p. 75). Secondly, there is the idea of struggle. Haggard rarely refers to 'struggle' in terms of the survival of the fittest; rather, he refers to a struggle for existence, insisting that life itself is a battle. The narrator of *Colonel Quaritch*, for example, adds a postscript to that brave gymnasium-world of Stevenson's:

A man's life is always more or less of a continual struggle; he is a swimmer upon an adverse sea, and to live at all he must keep his limbs in motion . . . We struggle for our livelihoods, and for all that makes life worth living in the material sense, and not the less are we called upon to struggle with an army of spiritual woes and fears, which now we vanquish and now are vanquished by.
(1888, p. 212)

In a similar passage in *Beatrice*, Beatrice tells Geoffrey that ' "Existence is not worth having unless one is struggling with something and trying to overcome it" ' (1892b, p. 13). In *Jess*, the narrator comments that 'nature . . . will allow of no standing still among her subjects, and has ordained that strife of one sort or another shall be the absolute condition of existence' (1889a, p. 80). The idea of a struggle offers not simply another view of the activist disposition and its cultivation of the vigorous and combative tone, but a reminder of the belligerence of Social Darwinist precepts.

Struggling with the intangible world of the spirit is a recurrent concern of Haggard's. It is this struggle to which Noot, Ayesha's philosopher-king, refers in *Wisdom's Daughter*:

'the human heart is a great battle where our higher and lower parts fight with spiritual spears and arrows, till one side or the other wins victory and flies the banner of good or evil, of Isis or Set. Only out of struggle comes perfectness; that which has never struggled is a dead creature from whom little may be hoped.'   (1923, pp. 52–3)

Struggle is the highest good of Haggard's own particular brand of stoicism. Regardless of the fact that intention or will may be at odds with fate, or that what is pursued as good may be its very opposite, struggle is obligatory. The only alternative to a code of struggle, or action, is passivity and death. Haggard's use of the term 'struggle', then, is not simply an imitation of Social Darwinist jargon.

One critic who advances quite different views of the ideas in Haggard's works as they relate to either the prescriptions of Social Darwinism in particular or imperialism in general is Alan Sandison. In *The Wheel of Empire*, Sandison sets out to prove that, far from being an advocate of vulgar Darwinism, Haggard is a cultural relativist. He argues that Haggard's perspective reflects a fatalism that is linked not to providential design, but its very opposite – 'a vast mechanistic process, ungoverned and ungovernable' (Sandison, 1967, p. viii). Reasoning that Haggard's 'deepening fear that humanity in all its racial compartments . . . might yet turn out to be the helpless subject' (1967, p. viii) of the mechanistic process of fate, Sandison also argues that Haggard was free of racial prejudice. In Sandison's hands, Haggard becomes nothing less than an enlightened imperialist:

On occasion he is, of course, to be found subscribing to a belief in Britain's imperial destiny. But there are very few traces of the familiar Victorian paternalism which contact with the "natives" normally elicited . . . [He] repudiates without fuss the whole arrogant notion of the white man's burden.
                                                   (1967, pp. 30–1)

Sandison supports his contention with an argument based on Haggard's cosmology; he isolates two operative words in Haggard's work, 'process' and 'purpose': 'The first acknowledges Haggard's acute feelings of things being in a state of flux and change, the second relates to his lasting preoccupation with the question of design in nature, with whether or not there was a Providence which ordered events' (1967, p. 26). Given the above concerns, Sandison sees that three possibilities were open to Haggard:

These were firstly that there *was* a principle of order in the universe and that it was dictated by God; secondly, that there *was* a principle of order in the universe, but its determination was purely mechanical with accident as its first cause; thirdly, that there was *no* order inherent in the universe and chance dominated all. There is, occasionally, the merest hint of an interesting fourth possibility – that what order there is in nature has been put there by man.   (1967, p. 26)

Haggard leans, he says, in the direction of pessimism. 'More precisely', Sandison continues, 'though the third seems at times to have a certain purchase, it is the second possibility which exercises the most powerful fascination over him' (1967, p. 26).

Given the relatively straightforward nature of a Haggard work, little room appears to exist for extreme divergence of opinion. Except, however, in the case of his most disreputable characters or his 'good' characters in their very bleakest of moments, when they say things they retract almost immediately, Haggard's work shows few signs of adhering to a theory of the universe which assumes no order and accepts the uncertainty of chance. As for a theory which supposes order without purpose, the evidence is heavily weighted to the contrary. Although Haggard toys with the idea of a universe devoid of meaning, he does so in the process of what he himself might call spiritual struggle, during which fears are revealed chiefly to be abandoned. Most of his efforts go to disproving such doubts and fears with which he seems to have been unable to live.

Sandison maintains that Haggard had a predilection for the second choice – order and accident. Herein lies Sandison's central point: 'for Haggard as for Darwin the crucial issue was the accidental variation from which species developed' (1967, p. 26). Sandison explains that Darwin's theory of natural selection from accidental variation leads to denial of purpose, which Haggard could not accept. So far, so good. What follows, however, is far from convincing:

Haggard's . . . inability to accept the Darwinian denial of purpose was not matched by any real confidence in the obvious alternative . . . In almost every

103

case pessimistic misgivings undermine his attempt to find consolation in a conjectural Divine Plan too great for man's puny intellect to grasp.

(1967, p. 27)

Haggard's uneasiness and misgivings about a beneficent Providence are undeniable, but it is equally true to say that *they* are constantly undermined by faith in a Divine Plan. It is difficult to tell by what device Sandison measures confidence; a standard instrument would indicate too much evidence to the contrary to support his view. Most of Haggard's characters faithfully and stubbornly adhere to a belief in a supreme power that directs their actions. Certainly Haggard was distressed by life's evident miseries and suffering, but he continued to rationalize and justify their existence.

Sandison summons as evidence Alston's remarks to Ernest in *The Witch's Head*, but these remarks deny divine cruelty rather than divine purpose, and are more provocative than definitive. Sandison also asserts that characters like Devene and Frank Müller, who believe in chaos and chance, speak with more conviction than a character like Rupert Ullershaw. But a critic cannot make a convincing argument by depending on the utterances of doubt and disbelief spoken by minor characters when the central and more affirmative characters carry the burden of their stories. Sandison further claims that Haggard's legacy from Darwin is a sense of process and change, a conviction that all is transitory. Accordingly, Haggard's agonizings over the unseen world demonstrate his belief in 'the subservience of all races, creeds and opinions to process and flux' (Sandison, 1967, p. 41). Moreover, Sandison suggests, this awareness of change prevents Haggard from supporting Social Darwinism. Haggard's interest in humankind and nature as part of the great evolutionary process, he proposes, is quite independent of and alien to themes of war and aggressive conflict.

Previous chapters have more than demonstrated Haggard's militant mentality, his racial consciousness, and his concern with national and racial degeneration. As for actual instances of Social Darwinism in Haggard, some do exist, as Sandison concedes. One is Ayesha's assertion that 'in this world none save the strongest can endure. Those who are weak must perish; the earth is to the strong, and the fruits thereof. For every tree that grows a score shall wither, that the strong one may take their share' (Haggard, 1957, p. 210).

But, it may be asked, are these views to be taken for Haggard's? It would seem so, judging from a letter Haggard wrote to *The Times* regarding the Matabele:

They drove out inferior races and are now, with more cause, driven out or rather conquered by a race superior to themselves. Savagery is doomed in the southern parts of Africa and it must go. This may seem a hard saying, but it is and will remain a true one till the lion lies down with the lamb and the earth ceases to be to the strong.   (6 November 1893, p. 8)

Contrary to Sandison's opinion, Haggard's awareness of change, as it is indicated in the letter, does not prevent him from believing, and advising others to believe, that strife is fundamental to life.

Sandison's major contention that Haggard could not accept denial of purpose but had no confidence in anything else requires further rebuttal. There are at least two examples in the fiction of Haggard's attempt to deal with the problem of doubt, one in *Stella Fregelius* and another in *Beatrice*. These give some idea of the way that Haggard transforms doubt into faith.

At the end of *Stella Fregelius*, Morris Monk comes across a section of Stella's diary which reveals that spiritual doubts had started to possess her after the death of her sister. She had begun to wonder whether people were not 'mere accidents, born of the will of the chance of the flesh, and shaped by the pressure of centuries of circumstance' (1904, p. 299) and whether all religions were not 'different forms of a gigantic fraud played by his own imagination upon blind, believing man' (1904, pp. 299–300). Sandison suggests that Stella is one of many principal characters who experience a 'failure to achieve a real fulfilment' (1967, p. 39). But achieving real fulfilment and achieving a sense of faith are not the same thing. Moreover, Stella's doubts, as Sandison neglects to mention, are subsequently overcome, and her diary stands as a record of spiritual faith. It remains a lesson to Morris:

In Stella he beheld an example of the doctrines of Christianity really inspiring the daily life of the believer. If her strong faith animated all those who served under that banner, then in like circumstances they would act as she had acted. They would have no doubts; their fears would vanish; their griefs be comforted...

Many things are promised to those who can achieve faith. Stella achieved it and became endued with some portion of the promise. Spiritual faith, not inherited, nor accepted, but hard-won by personal struggle and experience; that was the key-note to her character and the explanation of her actions.

(1904, pp. 322–3)

Left with this legacy, Morris too can follow the example of Stella's spiritual struggle.

A more pointed recounting of spiritual doubt and conversion comes in *Beatrice*. Beatrice, a freethinker who expresses an interest in Darwin and disavows Christianity, is spiritually transformed through her love for Geoffrey Bingham. The verbal exchange in which Geoffrey and Beatrice are charged with the task of airing the familiar aspects of the debate on belief as seen by Haggard is characteristically inconclusive. Geoffrey is allowed to respond to Beatrice's reference to worldly suffering by saying that ' "it is no argument . . . to point to the existence of evil and unhappiness among men as proof of the absence of a superior Mercy; for what are men that such things should not be with them?" ' (1892b, p. 119). He suggests that she look at nature for proof, and Beatrice replies in kind:

'all this reasoning drawn from material things does not touch me. That is how the Pagans made *their* religions, and it is how Paley strives to prove his. They argued from the Out to the In, from the material to the spiritual. It cannot be; if Christianity is true it must stand upon spiritual feet and speak with a spiritual voice, to be heard, not in the thunderstorm, but only in the hearts of men.'   (1892b, p. 120)

This insistence on an intuitive sensing of Christianity puts a considerable strain on Geoffrey's ability to argue. However, Beatrice's conversion comes as she said it must, naturally and intuitively, without any proof but her own subjective conviction. Grief-stricken when she thinks, mistakenly, that Geoffrey is dead, her faith is reborn 'and, as all human beings must in their hour of mortal agony, Beatrice realised her dependence on the Unseen' (1892b, p. 137). Later in the book she thinks back to her days of agnosticism 'before she learned to love, and hand in hand had seen faith and hope re-arise from the depths of her stirred soul' (1892b, p. 284).

Haggard's response to the evolutionary spirit of his time has little to do with its scientism, as has been shown, and much to do with its implications for faith. His own religious eclecticism finds a metaphorical correspondence with evolutionary theory in the idea of a mystical, spiritual evolution, the movement of the individual to God or an eternal oneness. Haggard's occasional endorsement of the notion of reincarnation is, in this regard, his own way of countering the misery of individual lives. This proclivity to mysticism is especially given to the character of Ayesha, who claims in *She* that 'we shall sleep . . . we shall awake and live again, and again shall sleep, and so on and on, through periods, spaces, and times, from aeon unto aeon, till the world is dead' (1957, p. 194). Haggard's undogmatic Christianity and his notion of spiritual evolution are both attempts to accommodate to evolutionary thought.

Haggard felt strongly the contradiction between a hypothetical Grand Design and the ostensible disorder of the world. The pattern that ordered the universe was not apparent in life. But the core of Haggard's fatalism is its axiomatic character; it depends upon faith, not reason. Faith, however, did not prevent Haggard from trying to understand the significance of the universe. His dabbling in spiritualism, Egyptology, and metempsychosis attests to that. In such works as *Stella Fregelius*, *She*, *Ayesha*, *Wisdom's Daughter*, *She and Allan*, and *The World's Desire*, he actively strives for some understanding of his world. Likewise, his fictional travels in Empire were journeys with spiritual or psychological motivation as well. These tales – in which geography is used symbolically and the secret of life, or 'the world's desire', is sought – always function at one level, as allegory. In order to better understand how Haggard deals with the contradictions between sacred order and profane chaos it is necessary to discuss next these periodic allegorical searches for greater understanding. This discussion should serve to translate his insistence on the supremacy of the spirit into terms of Empire.

Chapter 5

JEKYLL AND HYDE ABROAD: SCIENCE AND SPIRITUALISM

The remarkable thing about late-Victorian imperialism was its ability to satisfy both the spiritual and the material needs of the British. That the very same imperial venture could simultaneously minister to Britain's souls and fill its coffers while preserving a veneer of consistency throughout was no small achievement. Indeed, a more profitable undertaking would be difficult to imagine. Predictably, Haggard and his fellow romancers encouraged a view of Empire that virtually ignored its material reality. The matter-of-fact world of factories, ships, military equipment, loans, stock market investments and railways which sustained the Empire and the vast material wealth that created it were kept at a more than respectable distance from popular literary depictions of the phenomenon. Haggard's fiction in particular, with its emphatic spiritualism, was not only dissociated from this material side of things but altogether antithetical to it. To see the literature of Empire in perspective, therefore, it must be viewed against the seemingly incongruous background of balance sheets, technology, and a most immoderate greed.

The precondition for imperialism was Britain's entry into a machine economy with industrial methods of production. Imperial Britain's development as an advanced industrial nation was many times improved in the late nineteenth century during what is now referred to as the second industrial revolution or the revolution in the natural sciences.[1] Great changes in technology led to inventions in transportation and communication – two areas that lend themselves favourably to expansionist policies – as well as in industry. Thus, while many of the early Empire builders were truly rugged individualists, those in the latter half of the century and later were engineers and military men as well as skilled ranchers and planters. Even the imperial administrator, made famous by Kipling, was a product of this changing and increasingly bureaucratic society. The flamboyant adventurer-hunter-trader made famous by Haggard in his portrayal of Allan Quatermain was not, however, representative of this group, but he was none the less the most romantic figure on the imperial scene.

The changes introduced by scientific discovery were so irresistibly exciting that science quickly fell prey to the imagination of romance both within and without the field of literature. Cecil Rhodes's famous statement – that he would annex the planets if he could – attests to the expansively romantic side of this imperialist who, it is said, 'worshipped scientific development' (Hobman, 1955, p. 114). His dream of the Cape Town to Cairo railway is surely another bit of romantic, if aggressive, imperialism. The vision of a purer race, which captivated 'patriotic' eugenicists, is an indulgence of the same sort. And there is clearly nothing dispassionately scientific in the attitudes of Social Darwinism. Science can be easily pressed into the service of reaction, and it was readily gathered into the imperial fold.

Among Haggard's fellow romance enthusiasts, Kipling is probably the most renowned propagandist for the cause of the machine. C. E. Carrington claims that Kipling's 'McAndrew's Hymn' 'launched upon the world the new concept of the romance of machinery' (1970, p. 261), which he sees developed in Kipling's later stories as 'a sort of pantheism that felt the world-soul throbbing with life, even in railway engines and steamships' (1970, p. 261). The world of the machine, for Kipling, was also the world of work and action, bringing a sense of achievement and satisfaction.

Kipling's respect for the machine, however, exists alongside his regard for spiritualism and even mysticism, an uneasy association that is sometimes dissolved by conflicts dramatized as a confrontation between West and East. He was fascinated by spiritualism and magic, which is apparent in stories such as 'In the House of Suddhoo', 'Beyond the Pale', 'The Phantom Rickshaw', 'The Brushwood Boy', and 'They'. In fact, Kipling's attitude to science is occasionally quite critical, and his response to the industrial world was certainly not as unequivocal as one might suppose from 'McAndrew's Hymn'. Industrial England struck him as somehow unnatural, and he was often intent on making unfavourable comparisons between it and the colonies.

Eric Stokes commends Kipling for what he describes as 'his aim of restoring a balance to the over-urbanized, over-intellectualized industrial society by linking it in service with the underdeveloped world and renewing it spiritually by fresh contact there with Nature and "otherness"' (1972, p. 93). This explains, for Stokes, the revitalization of Kipling's reputation, which has gone on apace since Eliot's 1941 edition of Kipling's verse, and the critical disclaimers regarding his imperial sympathies. However, it is Eliot who, in the prefatory essay to that famous edition, offers the more convincing interpretation of Kipling, implicitly (if unintentionally) refuting such disclaimers when he says that Kipling had a

vision of the people of the soil. It is not a Christian vision, but it is at least a pagan vision – a contradiction of the materialistic view: it is the insight into a harmony with nature which must be reestablished if the truly Christian imagination is to be recovered by Christians. What he is trying to convey is . . . a point of view unintelligible to the industrialized mind. (1963, p. 33)

Although both Stokes and Eliot draw attention to the sharp antagonism between matter and spirit which all of Kipling's engineers cannot negate, it is Eliot who clarifies Kipling's strongly traditionalist, if not reactionary, strain by pointing to his 'vision of the people of the soil' and to the idea of a return to or a recovery of some past harmony with nature.

Unlike Kipling, Stevenson did not have to 'take up' science; he was born into it. Engineering had been a family profession for generations, and Stevenson studied engineering himself, although early on he broke with family tradition. Perhaps because science was not perceived as an alien power, Stevenson felt no need either to challenge it outright or to incorporate it, via the machine image, into his work. His ongoing interest in science, however, is well established, as is his regard for Darwin, Huxley, and Spencer, particularly as they affected his dissatisfaction with orthodox Christianity. But the limitations of science for Stevenson are clear as well. In his essay 'Pan's Pipes', for instance, he writes:

There will always be hours when we refuse to be put off by the feint of explanation, nick-named science, and demand instead some palpitating image of our estate, that shall represent the troubled and uncertain element in which we dwell, and satisfy reason by the means of art. Science writes of the world as if with the cold finger of a star-fish; it is all true; but what is it when compared to the reality of which it discourses? (1911, p. 184)

This passage indicates no distrust of science, but rather its decided inferiority to life, that which it examines, in its freshness, strength, and originality.

The limitations of science, however, were not so great that they could not be mitigated by its rich imaginative potential, hence the popularity of science fiction. In *Dr Jekyll and Mr. Hyde* (1886), science begets its own destroyer in the laboratory of the unbalanced Dr Jekyll, the pure animal embodied in Hyde. The primitive being that emerges in the character of Hyde is a personification of evil – Jekyll himself puts it in these terms in his statement of the case – but he is also a figure of degeneracy, a reversion to a former and lower stage of evolutionary development, as is implied in the description of his 'ape-like fury'. In Stevenson's interesting pre-Freudian construct of the human personality, it is science that disturbs the balance between amoral animality and the socially respectable consciousness, albeit science that is mixed with mysticism.

In his private life, Stevenson's interest in the unknown regions of the human psyche followed more legitimate paths, but paths that might have attracted Dr Jekyll himself. He was, in the 1870s, the secretary of the Edinburgh Psychical Society, and he later belonged to the London Society for Psychical Research. In 1891, five years before he died, he wrote to a friend from Vailima, 'I am at bottom a psychologist and ashamed of it' (1924, p. 57). His shame appears to have come from his undisguised fascination with evil. Like others in the period, he was drawn to the underside of matter, and it was not science, but the strength of this emotional nether world that frightened him. Confusion and distress regarding the relationship between things material and spiritual coloured his response to science. Unfortunately, his reaction to this confusion and distress contributed to strained theories of primitivism and, by extension, to distorted pictures of both subject peoples and their rulers in the world of Empire.

Another convert to spiritualism was Conan Doyle, who was schooled in the sciences long enough to graduate as a medical doctor. Although he eventually left his profession in order to write, his training remained with him in the form of a firm respect for scientific and rational thinking, as the Sherlock Holmes stories demonstrate. But Holmes is a strange character, and less than totally devoted to the world of analytic principles. When he is not working tirelessly on a case, he is sunk in pipe-smoking or drug-induced dreaminess in his rather exotic and claustrophobic London rooms. Holmes's London moods of contemplation and lassitude perhaps bear the signs of Conan Doyle's own need to seek beyond the realm of science. At any rate he did seek beyond it – his conversion to spiritualism occurred at the beginning of the Great War. Conan Doyle saw spiritualism, it should be said, as a scientific study, and he defended it on the basis of his own personal experiences and those of others, many of whom, he says, were 'of the first scientific brains in the world' (Nordan, 1966, p. 157). He spent the last years of his life crusading for the spiritualist cause and preaching on 'the scientific character of spiritualist dogma' (1966, p. 157). But the spiritualist movement itself was mainly an ideological counter to what was seen as the vile materialism of the day.

Even Andrew Lang, the man who seems the most divorced from science and the material world, managed to find room for the machine in *The Mark of Cain* (1886) and *The Disentanglers* (1902). According to Roger Lancelyn Green, however, the trappings of science in Lang's writings are fanciful rather than technological:

It is strange to find Lang, who professed to loathe all things mechanical, introducing submarines and wireless telegraphy at a time when these were in their infancy . . . but he seems to have been among the earliest story-tellers to hit upon the idea of using the latest scientific developments to replace the magical devices of the fairytale. (1946, pp. 198–9)

Although a 'flying machine' resolves the mystery plot in *The Mark of Cain*, the importance of the machine is diminished by the numerous anthropological elements in the book, science merely enhancing and not controlling the tale. On the whole, Lang gave science little more than a lukewarm welcome, preferring to believe that 'there are human faculties as yet unexplained, as yet inconsistent with popular scientific "materialism"' (Green, 1946, p. 72). Moreover, like Stevenson and Conan Doyle, Lang was keenly interested in psychical phenomena, and he was an active member of the Society for Psychical Research.

Henley, next to Kipling, seems the likeliest person to have granted the scientific age a cordial reception. Although the bulk of his poetry does not have the hard-boiled, aggressive style of his prose and is rather more tranquil and graceful than one might expect, the 'Hospital' verses as well as the much later 'A Song of Speed' afford a glimpse of his appreciation for the new science. In 'A Song of Speed' (1903), inspired by a ride in a Mercedes belonging to fellow imperialist Alfred Harmsworth, Henley uses the automobile as a point of departure from which to extol the inventive and imaginative capacity of artists and scientists alike. Comparing their creative ability, he sees both working under the mantle of a God who is

> Smiling as Whistler,
> Smiling as Kelvin,
> And Rodin and Tolstoi,
> And Lister and Strauss
> (That with his microbes,
> This with his fiddles!)
> Tugged at his fingers
> And worked out his meanings.   (1921b, p. 265)

But the automobile, it seems, is largely an instrument to bring about a world that 'Slips past like a dream/ Of Speed' (1921b, p. 265), speed being more important than the machine itself and furnishing the heady motion an activist would enjoy. It is not the precision and technology of the machine that is being admired so much as its blinding pace and hypnotic force.

Henley's minor enthusiasm for science, however, cannot be equated with an enthusiasm for a scientific perspective, something he would have associated with a vulgar and detestable materialism. A look at nineteenth-century history, Jerome Hamilton Buckley asserts, left Henley with the vision of 'a time-honoured idealism gradually smothered by an ascendant materialism' (1945, p. 139). In 'Concerning Atkins' (*Pall Mall Magazine*, 1900), Henley reflects on the change from idealism to materialism regretfully: 'We wanted to make money; and we made it ... We began to minimise our importance in the comity of peoples; to misread the results of our tremendous experience; to argue that our fathers had been common fools, and that our destiny was quite other than they believed' (p. 281). The peace that sets in at the end of *For England's Sake* oozes with the corruptive rot of materialist comfort:

> the nation, in a dream
> Of money and love and sport, hangs at the paps
> Of well-being, and so
> Goes fattening, mellowing, dozing, rotting down
> Into a rich deliquium of decay.   (Henley, 1921b, p. 240)

In the same poem, war is envisaged as a desirable force of spiritual regeneration. Such a critique of materialism is thus an oblique invitation to an aggressive imperialism.

Given Haggard's preoccupation with the world of the spirit, his own antagonistic response to the new wave of science to which Empire owed so huge a debt is not surprising. In Haggard's case, the attack on science is almost but not quite as severe as his attack on materialism, the former being tainted by its association with the latter. Science was to be appreciated even though it was inferior in all ways to matters of the spirit. It was questionable chiefly when it came in the form of religious scepticism. It was thoroughly reprehensible, however, when it took shape as an all-pervasive philosophical outlook.

Materialism, the philosophical progeny of science, was to be despised. Haggard's inclination to reject or suspect materialism of any type follows from his spiritual determinism. A commonplace of his fiction is the polarization, in various forms, of spirit and matter. Set against the background of his age, he seems both more old-fashioned than his contemporaries in his apprehensive views of science and materialism and more representative of a period absorbed as it was in spiritualism, mysticism, and the unconscious, intuited world. In defending an Empire that rested so squarely on its material wealth, Haggard could do little else but engage in fraudulent idealization.

Haggard's most frequent objections are to the form of materialism which usually carries connotations of egotism, selfishness, and utter philistinism. Although his criticisms are often aimed at the petty vulgarisms of the *nouveau riche*, he objects more seriously to an egotism that is in direct contradiction with ideas of service, sacrifice, and duty, equating materialism with an ethical unscrupulousness. Fundamentally, however, his objections, whether voiced as such or not, are philosophical. As a philosophy, materialism upholds the primacy of matter and sense perception and supports the view that non-material ideas are reflections of the material world. In addition, the path to progress for its adherents is material. This Haggard could not abide.

Spiritualism, Haggard's own philosophical habit of mind, is a form of idealism and as such is materialism's opposite number. For the idealist, it is the spiritual or non-material world that is primary, and the path to progress for its adherents is spiritual or moral. Idealism, as

H. Stuart Hughes points out, was part of the German philosophic tradition, whereas the Anglo–French tradition favoured empiricism (1958, p. 184). And while the British, like the French, had gone the way of utilitarianism, positivism, democracy, and natural science, they had been influenced by the Germans in the late eighteenth and early nineteenth centuries, and were so again from about the 1880s to the 1914–18 war. Hughes suggests that the positivist tradition was too strong to be severely threatened by transplanted idealist thought, but it is fair to say that idealism, whether imported or home-grown, was none the less a central element in the manner of thought that prevailed during the age of Empire. For the purposes of this discussion, spiritualism will be seen as a combative philosophy, fighting sundry types of materialism and throwing suspicion on scientific explanations of natural phenomena. In effect, Haggard's philosophy situates the locus of all power in a spirit or idea and creates, implicitly, a fertile ground for tyranny. Translated into terms of Empire, spiritualism comes to suggest the non-material source of power that rules.

We have already seen that Haggard's faith in some spiritual entity depended on his belief in the inadequacy of the human mind to fathom the universal spirit. In his works Haggard dwells lengthily on this inadequacy and on the generally debilitating and fearful state of mind that accompanies it. In his view, the fear and unhappiness that is perpetuated by ignorance can be alleviated, significantly, only by faith, and those people who try to break through the impenetrable veil of the spirit discover only terrifying danger. What happens to Haggard's characters who attempt the break is usually tragic, and Haggard cautions against all such daring. Like the Zulu goddess Nomkhubulwana, who was forbidden from the sight of her worshippers, Ayesha is swathed in gauzy material and hidden from the people she rules. They are not only forbidden to see her, but they are also filled with dread by threats of the horrible dangers that lie beneath her cover. As Ayesha says of herself in *She*, 'Beauty is like lightening; it is lovely, but it destroys' (1957, p. 165). Ludwig Horace Holly and Leo Vincey, who leave England to find Ayesha, must be fully prepared for the unveiling of her blinding beauty, and although they stand up to the test remarkably well, Leo withers and dies after his first kiss. Ayesha is the most extreme case in Haggard of the spirituality that is often attributed to secular rule.

The source of Ayesha's deification is her supposed knowledge of the animating centre of the world: she has bathed in the fire of life. Although herself subject to a superior will, she is the visible manifestation of unknown spiritual depths. Her spiritual gifts are impressive: she commands a certain power of vision, produces spectacular visions for others, and possesses the secret to eternal life. But she is no conjuror and eschews anything to do with magic, a skill involving control of the objective world. (Compared with Zikali, the wizard whose evil derives from his efforts to gain control by magical trickery, Ayesha is an obviously superior being.) To Haggard, magic is a presumption, an attempt to control the uncontrollable.

This is not to say that Haggard's characters are resigned to their unenlightened state. Far from it. Haunted and overwhelmed by the desire for spiritual knowledge, Quatermain travels to the underworld in *She and Allan*. With Ayesha's help, he passes beyond the temporal world to become a disembodied spirit encountering the spirits of other dead souls, those both of his own life and of former forgotten lives. The journey is personally unsatisfying: 'I had seemed to descend, or ascend, into Hades, and there had only seen things that gave me little joy and did but serve to reopen old wounds' (1921, p. 284). It does, however, yield its measure of predictable insights. He learns that the body is housed in spirit, not spirit in the body; that 'truth' is contained within oneself, although it is very difficult to perceive; and that the human being is a hopelessly vain creature. If these seem hardly worth the trip, they are all a mere man, an alien figure in the world of the dead, will ever find. All in all, the journey is a bitter experience.

The lesson to be learned from *She and Allan* is stated best by Haggard himself in his autobiography:

> Mysticism in moderation adds a certain zest to life and helps to lift it above the level of the commonplace. But it is at best a dangerous sea to travel before the time. The swimmer therein will do well to keep near to this world's sound and friendly shore lest the lights he sees from the crest of those bewildering phantom waves should madden or blind him, and he sink, never to rise again.
>
> (1926a, II, p. 172)

The quest for spiritual knowledge is limited by one's mortality and involves psycho–spiritual hazards that exceed physical ones. The potential hazards of flirting with otherworldly phenomena constitute Haggard's reiterated caveat to mortals who are simply incapable of capturing the essence of the spiritual world.

In *Stella Fregelius*, an object lesson on the perils of excessive spiritual investigation, Morris Monk is physically destroyed by his efforts to reach the spiritual world. Like Dr Jekyll, Morris Monk is a scientist who tampers with the unknown, only in Monk's case the body dissipates rather than expands. Initially he dreams of making a sort of telepathic communications device. An electrical engineer turned physicist, he sets about his work as a scientist might, devising an invention called the aerophone. According to Haggard, the main motive for including the aerophone 'was to suggest how powerless are all such material means to bring within mortal reach the transcendental and unearthly ends which, with their aid, were attempted by Morris Monk' (1904, p. viii). In the end, the new province of knowledge that Morris Monk opens is disastrous.

After Stella Fregelius's death, Morris's ruling passion is to reach her spirit, and he is immediately burdened with the inadequacy of his scientific training:

> Wonderful as were his electrical appliances, innumerable as might be their impalpable emanations, insoluble as seemed the mystery of their power of catching and transmitting sounds by the agency of ether, they were still physical appliances producing physical effects in obedience to the laws of nature. But what he sought lay beyond nature and was subject to some rule of which he did not even know the elements, and much less the axioms. Herein his instruments, or indeed, any that man could make, were as futile and as useless as would be the prayers of an archbishop addressed to a Mumbo-jumbo in a fetish house. The link was wanting; there was, and could be, no communication between the two. The invisible ether which he had subdued to his purposes was still a constituent part of the world of matter; he must discover the spiritual ether, and discover also the animating force by which it might be influenced. (1904, p. 334)

Morris finally seizes upon a passage in Stella's diary which suggests that refining one's senses to an unnaturally heightened pitch will enable one to make contact with the spiritual world, and he begins to travel along a dangerously suicidal path.

For Haggard, Morris Monk's cultivation of his spiritual self is not unlike the zealous attempts of seers and interpreters of oracles to mortify the flesh, and the consequences are similar as well:

> This is the rule: to beat down the flesh and its instincts and nurture the spirit, its aspirations and powers. And this is the end – to escape ... into an

atmosphere of vision true or false, where human feet were meant to find no road, and trammelled minds of men no point of outlook.   (1904, p. 335)

Morris sits up night after night trying to communicate with the spirit of Stella. In time he begins to have visions, but by then he has been driven so insane by his efforts that he can scarcely be considered to have a physical existence. He weakens and dies. For the reader, Haggard leaves the familiar reminder that 'To attempt to draw the last veil from the face of Truth in any of her thousand shapes is surely a folly and predoomed to failure' (1904, p. 339).

In book after book Haggard affirms the inviolability and supremacy of the spirit, the vulnerability of materialism, and the opposition of both. In *The Ghost Kings*, Rachel Dove, the incarnation of the divine Inkosazana, is opposed to the perversely materialist Ishmael. Ishmael, having lived among Africans long enough to absorb certain of their beliefs, falls madly in love with Rachel because, 'she was beautiful, which appealed to his strong animal nature, and spiritual, which appealed to a materialist soaked in Kaffir superstition' (1908, p. 131). The dramatic polarities in Haggard's historical novel *Pearl Maiden* (1903) are Miriam, the faithful Catholic, and Caleb, the Jew, who 'was unable to divine that mind is greater than matter, while spirit is greater than mind; and that in the end, by many slow advances and after many disasters seemingly irremediable, spirituality will conquer all' (1903, p. 75).

In *Benita*, the antagonism between the rapacious Jacob Meyer and the clairvoyant Benita Clifford, who retains the spirit of a woman three hundred years dead, is basically the same. Jacob Meyer, another character given shape by Haggard's anti-semitism, has materialism in his blood:

He told her [Benita] that he was a German by birth, that he had been sent to England as a boy, to avoid the conscription, which Jews dislike, since in soldiering there is little profit. Here he had become a clerk in a house of South African merchants, and, as a consequence – having shown all the ability of his race – was despatched to take charge of a branch business in Cape Colony...   (1965a, p. 59)

The racial stereotype becomes a point of convergence for all of Haggard's aversions – the petty merchant mentality, the single-minded profit orientation, and the unpatriotic evasion of military service. No doubt Haggard had heard stories of moneyed South

African Jews, but they were not the source of his anti-semitism, since this was already well nurtured, serving coincidentally to complement his attack on materialism.

In addition to the methodically dramatized conflict between matter and spirit, Haggard persistently attempts to erode the authority of science and a materialist world-view and to call into question any tendency to scepticism. To this end, he frequently subverts science, materialism, and scepticism by the authority of experience. That is, those characters who must 'see' things to believe them do indeed come to witness all sorts of fantastic phenomena that defy rational explanation. The handling of Quatermain's character reveals this method to perfection, since Quatermain is continually represented as a pragmatic man whose serious misgivings about strange phenomena disappear following bizarre but thoroughly convincing experiences. In *The Ancient Allan* (1920), Quatermain meets a botanical scientist whose experience with mind-expanding drugs known to a tribe of South American Indians has challenged his own scientific views. Quatermain refuses to believe this otherwise sensible man, and the remainder of the book relates Quatermain's experience under the influence of Taduki, an African herb, which severely shakes his disbelief. He is taken back thousands of years and becomes an ancient Egyptian hunter and noble.

Ironically, Quatermain is the most 'scientific' of Haggard's characters, thus making his fall from reason all the more convincing. He even disavows being a party to romance: in *She and Allan*, for example, at a point when he finds himself in a particularly tight spot, he cautions his readers against thinking that he leads a charmed life, 'that everything will happen as it ought to do if this were a romance instead of a mere record of remarkable facts' (Haggard, 1921, p. 205). This obvious bit of banter is one passage of many that insist on a fidelity to history; in fact, many of the Quatermain stories actually pretend to be edited memoirs.

The style and significance of the Quatermain pose is wittily described by Morton Cohen in a passage that merits lengthy quotation:

Quatermain believes in scientific realism: all unusual phenomena must be proved before he will believe them. This is not a world of cock-and-bull ghost stories, of fairies and wraiths – this is a man's world, and science is a man's tool for proving or disproving. From the outset Quatermain is a hard-headed cynic

119

who has no use for humbug, will not tolerate magical hocus-pocus, and absolutely abhors superstition . . . He is, in a word, a sceptic, and since he usually is the teller of the tales, he tells them from a sceptical point of view . . . And then suddenly (but never too soon), the sceptic comes face to face with the impossible, the imponderable, and his reaction is just what we would expect: he does not believe what he sees. But there it is before him, and he looks for some explanation. He subjects the phenomenon to all the tests of reason: Ayesha is after all there before his own eyes, and her story is air-tight; King Solomon's treasure is not something he imagines: he runs his fingers through the cold, glittering gems. Perhaps, dear reader, the sceptic is forced to suggest, there is more in heaven and earth than is dreamt of in our scientific realism. (1968, p. 222)

This good-humoured account of the journey over the bridge of scepticism not only elucidates the Quatermain pose, but it also underscores the importance of the 'experience'. Latent spiritualism is sparked into life by the irrefutable experience, and the experience becomes the basis for truth. Although readers are not actually encouraged to believe that the inconceivable events and phenomena which Haggard's characters confront are much more than the fruit of a highly prolific imagination, they are certainly urged to consider the wisdom of lowering their credibility threshold and remaining open to the possible revelations of the infinite and mysterious totality of life. So Haggard, with formula in hand, sets up his own anomalous mobile laboratory, as it were, and goes to work testing scepticism, science, and materialism, only to have them overcome by the potency of the spirit.

By far the most incredible test occurs in 'Smith and the Pharaohs' (1912–13), a story serialized in the *Strand Magazine* in which Haggard was able to make use of his interest in Egyptian archaeology. With ill-concealed suspicion, the narrator begins the story by setting forth the case of science as regards its sovereignty in the area of human knowledge, the tone being very definitely, if gently, polemical:

Scientists . . . tell us they know all that there is worth knowing about man, which, of course, includes woman. They trace him from his remotest origins; they show us how his bones changed and his shape modified, also how, under the influence of his needs and passions his intelligence developed from something very humble. They demonstrate conclusively that there is nothing in man which the dissecting-table will not explain; that his aspirations towards another life have their root in the fear of death, his affinities with the past are merely inherited from remote ancestors who lived in that past, perhaps a million years ago; and that everything noble about him is but the fruit of expediency or of a veneer of a civilization . . . Man, in short, is an animal. Such are the facts, they (or some of them) declare. (1981, p. 148)

The trap is set; experience lies waiting in ambush. Suddenly, he continues, 'something comes within the range of our experience which gives us pause and causes doubts . . . to arise again deep in our hearts, and with them a yet diviner hope' (1981, p. 148). The story proper then unfolds with its edifying specimen of unexplainable, unaccountable experience. Smith, who has inconveniently fallen in love with the plaster cast of an unknown woman in Egyptian sculpture in the British Museum, travels to Egypt and finds the original head of the statuette in a tomb. He later gets locked in the Cairo Museum after hours and is privileged to witness, among the mummies, an annual gathering of Egyptian kings and queens whose spirits reinhabit their bodies. Here the woman of the sculpture acknowledges him as the incarnation of a former lover. Smith, a totally prosaic and unprepossessing man, suddenly 'awakens' and wonders whether his experience was real or just a dream. A line from an earlier part of the story lingers: 'Perchance when all is said . . . man is something more than an animal . . . Perhaps the dream is true' (1981, p. 148).

In *The Yellow God*, Haggard presents still another character whose scepticism and materialist outlook need shaking up. Aylward, a financier, explains his contemptuous record of pondering only the tangible just at the point when his views are being challenged by incontrovertible experience:

I am a man who has never believed in anything I cannot see and test, one who utterly lacks faith. In my leisure I have examined into the various religious systems, and found them to be rubbish. I am convinced that we are but highly-developed mammals born by chance, and when our day is done, departing into the bleak nothingness out of which we came. Everything else, what is called the higher and spiritual part, I attribute to the superstitions incident to the terror of the hideous position in which we find ourselves, that of gods of a sort hemmed in by a few years of fearful and tormented life.

(1909, p. 78)

When a gold statue, the yellow god of the book's title, 'swims' across the floor of his office, he is understandably confused. 'And now', he says, 'I am confronted with an experience which I cannot explain' (1909, p. 78). Inexplicable perhaps, but not without significance: the moving statue correctly portends Aylward's death.

Yet another instance of this challenge from experience appears in *Benita*, the object of its assault being the odious Jacob Meyer, who denies Benita's claim to have communed with the spirit of an ancient Portuguese woman. In an explanation that shows him to be less of a materialist than either he, Benita, or their creator thinks, Meyer argues that Benita was animated by her subconscious. However inadequate as an account of Benita's sudden fluency in Portuguese, it fails to expose any chinks in Meyer's wall of opposition. ' "When I see a spirit and know that it is a spirit" ', he insists, ' "then doubtless I shall believe in spirits" ' (1965a, p. 181). Finally he does see a spirit, is maddened by the experience, and dies.

Were it not for a sort of campy humour that infects the more preposterous 'experiences' he stage-manages, Haggard's attempts to discredit scepticism and materialism would be far more tedious than they are. For readers who can temporarily disregard general notions of taste, *When the World Shook* (1919) will prove highly amusing. In this book, another hymn to spirituality, Haggard introduces an earnest if confused seeker of truth named Arbuthnot and his decidedly uncon-fused friends, Bickley and Bastin, representatives of, respectively, science and religion. To Bickley, life is 'merely a short activity bounded by nothingness before and behind' (1919b, p. 24), and man is a 'brute-descended accident and no more' (1919b, p. 15). Bickley is irredeemably optimistic about understanding the nature of the world – 'everything inexplicable has a perfectly mundane explanation' (1919b, p. 15) – and slavishly devoted to Haggard's bugaboo, chance. The phlegmatic Bastin, on the other hand, rules that life is nothing more than the prelude to 'golden-harped and haloed immortality' (1919b, p. 24). As the narrator of the piece and, like Haggard himself, more mystical than religious, Arbuthnot suggests that life is perhaps

something quite different from [what] either of these [interpretations allow], something vast and splendid beyond the reach of vision, something God-sent, beginning and ending in the Eternal absolute and at last partaking of attributes and nature from aeon to aeon shot through with His light.

(1919b, p. 24)

His uncertainty is put to the dependable test of experience.

In search of what is never actually specified and seems to result from a conversation about a picture of an underdressed Pacific Island woman whose charms are about the one thing all three can agree upon, the men find themselves on a South Sea island. They soon discover the non-airtight coffins of an old man and young woman entombed in a cave and, oddly enough, the bodies have not yet decayed. Oro, the man, is roused by an injection of strychnine which Bickley happens to have handy, and Yva, the woman, stirs after the man waves his arms over her body. They explain that they have been asleep for 250,000 years. The veteran Haggard reader is unimpressed, but Bickley, the intractable scientist, is incredulous. He demands that the implausible story, indeed the entire 'experience', be rejected, insisting that since the ' "experience is not natural, and everything in the Universe so far as we know, has a natural explanation, I am inclined to believe that we are suffering from hallucinations" ' (1919b, p. 138). The reader sneers knowingly at his disbelief.

The best is yet to follow. Oro, it emerges, was formerly part of a once great civilization called The Sons of Wisdom, and he quickly assesses Bickley, of whose scepticism he is contemptuous, as a ' "little man of science, who because [he sees] the face of things, thinks that [he knows] the body and the heart" ' (1919b, p. 181). Naturally enough, Oro wants to take stock of the new world he has just re-entered, and somehow manages to transport himself and Arbuthnot to London, then a city in the throes of the First World War. Parliament, a Trafalgar Square labour riot, a restaurant, and a dance hall are all roundly condemned (only a Salvation Army meeting gains approval). Finding the world so manifestly deficient in virtue, Oro attempts to alter the earth's balance by tampering with a giant mechanism in its bowels and is prevented only at the last moment by Yva, who has fallen in love with Arbuthnot. At the end of the adventure Arbuthnot dies quite suddenly, having reached no conclusions about the nature of 'truth'. But by then any conclusion would be a superfluous validation of what has already been proven: science has no monopoly on knowledge and indeed can tell us little about the well-springs of life.

Of all the parables of the division between the spirit and the flesh in Haggard's works, the Ayesha stories are the most rewarding of attention. Ayesha herself, 'daughter of Wisdom yet Folly's slave' (1923, 'Editor's Note'), is a very victim of the clash between the spirit and the flesh, or more precisely, of Isis and Aphrodite. According to Ayesha's vision of her former life as high-priestess to Isis, the temples of her goddess were being deserted for those of Aphrodite, and Ayesha's own loyalty was soon to become her undoing. Aphrodite decides to punish her through Kallikrates, a priest of Isis with whom Ayesha falls in love. She curses Ayesha with a love for him that is to be unsatisfied 'till the world's end' (1921, p. 164), and warns her victim against any false hopes for deliverance: ' "Think not that thou shalt escape my doom, for know that however strong the spirit, here upon the earth the flesh is stronger still and of all flesh I am the queen" ' (1921, p. 164). When Ayesha falls down in the temple of Isis to pray to Aphrodite, she incurs the wrath of Isis in turn and is doomed to years of lonely waiting and suffering until the reincarnation of her lover: ' "Moreover" ', Isis tells her, ' "through it all thou shalt despise thyself, which is man's and woman's hardest lot, thou who having the rare feast of spirit spread out before thee, hast chosen to fill thyself from the troughs of flesh" ' (1921, p. 125). Eventually, Isis promises, she shall be lifted from her torment and rejoined with her lover. The very personification of the problem that plagues most of Haggard's characters, Ayesha is also closer to the secret of life than any other.

While Haggard's presentation of the eternal disjunction of matter and spirit in its various forms points to nothing so specific as an expansionist ideology, it does suggest something about the nature of power, as it is understood by Haggard, and ultimately translates into political terms. Many of its implications should be fairly clear by now: if the locus of all ruling power is in a spirit or idea, this supreme spiritual mandate (or fate) requires neither justification nor rationality in its practical execution. Regardless of who wields power, ageless *femmes fatales* like Ayesha or ordinary Englishmen like Allan Quatermain, its source is in the unseen spiritual world. In addition to the echoes of 'divine will' with which this emphasis on spirituality resounds, there are other and more subtle implications having to do with the psychology of power, its potential for the nurturing of fear and terror, its capacity for manipulation, and its easily stirred infatuation with tyranny.

It would seem logical to assume, if the source of all knowledge as well as its power resides in the spiritual world, that the spirit that moves people to act is endowed with some sort of superior consciousness or will. But the superiority of this spiritual consciousness is no guarantee of its sense of charity, and its open-endedness allows for a whimsical inconsistency: one cannot define the form or the limits of such a vague spiritual entity, and its formlessness and limitlessness have in themselves the potential for either creativity or vast destruction. One hazards a chance on the kindness of one's fate and lives with insecurity. Haggard was not unaware of the fear inspired by spiritual rule, and he does not fail to notice the extremes to which spiritual rule can be extended, most explicitly in his conception of Ayesha and her empire at Kôr.

V. S. Pritchett, who appears to have no doubts about the psychological resonances of Haggard's work, suggests that Haggard tapped the most hidden longings and appetites of the English people: 'Mr E. M. Forster once spoke of the novelist sending down a bucket into the unconscious; the author of *She* installed a suction pump. He drained the whole reservoir of the people's secret desires' (1960, p. 277). Among them, Pritchett submits, were fantasies of omnipotence: 'in an empire-building age, [he drew] on fantasies of absolute spiritual rule in secret cities' (1960, p. 277). Pritchett is certainly on solid ground in the case of the 'She' or Ayesha books, of which there are four, *She* (1887), *Ayesha* (1905), *She and Allan* (1921), and *Wisdom's Daughter* (1923). She-who-must-be-obeyed, the beautiful white queen who ruled in the heart of Africa, has powers that are both immense and seductively inviting. Nina Auerbach, who includes Ayesha in her remarks on late Victorian queens in *Woman and the Demon*, sees Ayesha as 'Haggard's version of a national myth' (1982, p. 37), that is, Victoria, and suggests the possibility of 'aligning Haggard's magic country alarmingly with his reader's expanding national reality' (1982, p. 37). The numerous and conspicuously female rulers in Haggard's fiction deserve a discussion of their own, but we can say at least that these women appear to function as 'outsider' figures who are more susceptible to indulgent and even lavish fantasies of power than Haggard's rather wooden and conventional male figures.

A good deal of Ayesha's attraction is created by her extreme wilfulness – she does whatever she wishes, regardless of the consequences. In point of fact, her Empire is not a model to emulate. She is ruthless to the Amahagger, her subjects, but they are barbarians, after all, and there is some suggestion that she cannot be totally blamed for treating them as she does. A character often seen as the psychological archetype of the immortal woman, she is possibly more interesting as an unconscious reflection of Haggard's ambivalence to authority (to say nothing of his sexual fantasies). She is, after all, not the stoical and well-disciplined Englishman – although there is some of him in her too – but a more complex sort of leader, more aware of the sheer pleasures of power and very much more terrifying. At the same time, she is practically irresistible. Holly explains her addictive effect in *She*: 'We could no more have left her than a moth can leave the light that destroys it. We were like confirmed opium-eaters: in our moments of reason we knew the deadly nature of pursuit, but certainly we were not prepared to abandon its terrible delights' (1957, p. 246). In his conception of Ayesha, Haggard shows his awareness of the corrupt and demonic aspect of rule by spiritual prerogative, the intoxication of expansion, and the imposition of social controls on a people by the ideological, or mythological, rendering of the divine mission.

Haggard's ambivalence to authoritarian rule reveals itself in the irreconcilable quarrels between Ayesha, the autocrat, and Holly and Vincey, the English democrats. One of these occurs in *She*, after Ayesha decides that Leo Vincey ought to rule Britain and have the queen overthrown. She is shocked to learn that the English truly love their monarch, and she listens to them describe the nature of the monarchy and the state of democracy in England:

Again we explained that ... the sovereign under whom we lived was venerated and beloved by all right-thinking men ... Also, we told her that real power in our country rested in the hands of the people; that, in fact, we were ruled by the votes of the lower and least educated classes of the community. (1957, p. 258)

This democracy, Ayesha perceives, is itself vulnerable to tyranny: ' "Ah", she said, "democracy – then surely there is a tyrant, for I have long since seen that democracies, having no clear will of their own, in the end set up a tyrant, and worship him" ' (1957, p. 258). Holly agrees that tyrants do indeed exist in England, and Ayesha returns to her original suggestion. Realizing that Ayesha is, as she says, 'above the law' (1957, p. 259), Holly expects that one day she will control Britain and the world:

In the end she would, I had little doubt, assume absolute rule over the British dominions, and probably over the whole earth, and, though I was sure that she would speedily make ours the most glorious and prosperous empire that the world had ever seen, it would be at the cost of a terrible sacrifice of life.

(1957, pp. 259–60)

The price of the most glorious and prosperous empire, Holly appears to realize, is exorbitant, but he is not completely outraged by it:

I could only conclude that this marvellous creature . . . was now about to be used by Providence as a means to change the order of the world, and possibly, by the building up of a power that could no more be rebelled against or questioned than the decrees of Fate, to change it materially for the better.

(1957, p. 260)

Not only is Holly willing to accept a more ruthless rule as the divine hand of Providence once again, but he is also willing to entertain the idea that the control and prevention of rebellion that Ayesha's type of rule promises might well be an improvement. It is not unreasonable to speculate that Haggard was just as fearful of democracy as he was of despotism.

Disagreements over the limits of power reappear in *Ayesha*, in which the plan to take over Britain is superseded by a plan to rule the world, with Leo Vincey installed as absolute monarch. Vincey, 'a hater of absolute monarchies and somewhat republican in his views and sympathies' (1905, p. 289), clearly represents the incarnation of British sobriety and disapproves of this scheme for global hegemony. He assures her that 'he desired no such empire' (1905, p. 286). But if Vincey fails to be captivated by the idea of such vast power, Ayesha positively radiates excitement at the prospect: ' "it will please me, to see Powers, Principalities and Dominions, marshalled by their Kings and governors, bow themselves before our thrones and humbly crave the liberty to do our will" ' (1905, p. 287). Holly, considering her ambitions to be 'such as no imperial-minded madman could conceive' (1905, p. 289), is stupefied by her insatiable appetite for power.

Some modification of this almost demonic aspect of Ayesha is made later on in the book when she offers Leo and Holly a glimpse of the good life under her rule. The merchant, the money lender, and the fortune seeker of the international stock exchanges – Haggard's despised materialists – would be made most uncomfortable in her domain. Ayesha, it seems, would prefer the simplicity of barter to the rather more complex system of commodity exchange based on gold and, in her view, greed:

'when the nations are beggarded [sic] and their golden god is down; when the usurer and the fat merchant tremble and turn white as chalk because their hoards are but useless dross; when I have made the bankrupt Exchanges of the world my mock, and laugh across the ruin of its richest markets, why, then, will not true worth come to its heritage again?

'What if I do discomfort those who think more of self than of courage and virtue . . .? What if I uphold the cause of the poor and the oppressed against the ravening lusts of Mammon? Why, will not this world of yours be happier then?' (1905, pp. 300–1)

By having Ayesha challenge the authority of gold, Haggard has significantly diminished the malevolence of her rule, if not drawn her into his own camp altogether. If Ayesha's ambition to rule the world is outrageous, her sentiments, at least, are not.

Although Ayesha is a cruelly capricious leader who has taken great liberties with the Amahagger – her diversions include the selective breeding of the Amahagger to dwarfs, giants, musicians, and docile mutes – she manages to contain rebellion and anarchy. And, in her divine wisdom, she has managed the situation with relatively little force. Her methods of control are indeed fascinating, since they suggest that Haggard understood very well the ideological dimensions of imperialist rule or, specifically, the conversion of British supremacy into an image of invulnerability. The Ayesha stories depart sufficiently from the Quatermain tales to escape immediate identification with Empire, but they are also sufficiently concerned with the nature of power to comment indirectly on Haggard's own imperial views. Ayesha, then, is not so much an imperialist as she is an inspired woman who understands the art of state control, and she can manage and subjugate her people with expert skill. Her energies go to building an empire on her spiritual supremacy and coercing loyalty by her image of moral and spiritual superiority.

In *She*, for example, Ayesha condemns some of the Amahagger to death by torture for attacking Holly and Vincey and attempting to kill their servant. When Holly tries to intervene on behalf of her victims, Ayesha remains firm, explaining the rationale of her methods: ' "How thinkest thou that I rule this people? I have but a regiment of guards to do my bidding, therefore it is not by force. It is by terror. My empire is of the imagination" ' (1957, p. 184). The advantages of such an empire are clear; one needs no extensive military machine if obedience is so easily assured by terrifying images of torture and death.

But the tenuousness of such an empire is evident as well. If for one moment the vulnerability of its despotism were exposed, its existence would be cut short. The might of Ayesha's empire, then, is as imaginary as its method of control.

The dependence on imaginary superiority is referred to again in *Ayesha*, in which Vincey's disinclination for world power stems in part from his aversion to unnecessary bloodshed and war. Ayesha attempts to satisfy her own lust for power and, at the same time, allay Vincey's fears by convincing him of the possibility of a bloodless coup. Once more, her weapon is the imagination: 'When we appear among men, scattering gold to satisfy their want, clad in terrifying power, in dazzling beauty and in immortality of days, will they not cry, "Be ye our monarchs and rule over us!"' (1905, p. 288). Similarly, in *Wisdom's Daughter*, she explains that her power over the Amahagger is inspirational, if spiritual: ' "They were my slaves who feared me as a spirit, and I was kind to them, but if they angered me, then I slew them" ' (1923, p. 281). And, in *She and Allan*, the source of her might is quickly understood by Quatermain, who remarks that her power over the Amahagger 'was of a purely moral nature, one that emanated from her personality alone' (1921, p. 188). Quatermain's comment is admittedly more generous in effect, for it suggests a rule not of terror but of ethical superiority. But the righteousness of Ayesha – and Quatermain's ambivalence towards her originates in some such element of her personality – is inspired by fear. Although it is a fear of the kind that is associated with spiritual sovereignty and religious awe, it remains a coercive force.

The Ayesha books reveal Haggard's awareness of the way in which ideas and images of spiritual superiority can be effective political tools. An image of invincibility maintained the mystery and the sanctity of the alien ruler and kept the colonized peoples at a safe distance. In *Heu-Heu*, Haggard has Quatermain remark on the importance of preserving the psychological barrier between blacks and whites: 'Be as much afraid as you like, but never show fear before a native; if you do, your infuence over him is gone. You are no longer the great White Chief of higher blood and breeding; you are just a common fellow like himself' (1924, p. 11). White rulers cannot afford to be exposed; their image is their defence. William Thornton suggests in his *Doctrines of Imperialism* that such barriers prevented any genuine understanding between ruler and ruled. Built to ensure

British inviolability, they also prevented the attainment of even the purported 'civilizing' goals of the imperialists. The idea of social superiority, Thornton writes, precluded 'transmission of genuine ideals that were conceived by genuinely civilized men . . . For in the average European dependency, the native races were never admitted to the mental life of their masters' (1965, p. 197). It is difficult to believe that the creation of a mental barrier between the imperialists and their subjects was not intentional.

The extraordinary image of infallibility found in the Ayesha stories captures what is most troubling about Haggard's spiritualism. With its frightening potential to terrorize and subdue recalcitrant peoples, this façade of invincibility is quite in keeping with the needs of this most competitive phase of British imperialism that preceded the First World War. No longer did the Empire have the unhindered latitude that permitted, and even encouraged, the mid-century mood of zeal and optimism. National rivalry demanded new weapons of control: the Africans had to be made to fear the British (and likewise, the British had to be made to fear the Germans). But the explicit propagandistic use to which such an image of spiritual infallibility could be put identifies only the most utilitarian feature of Haggard's spiritualism. In less tangible terms, it must be seen as a philosophy which nurtures an enthusiasm for power and authority. For many of Haggard's readers, the passive watchers of their world, *She* more than likely provided restitution for a life of monotony and convention. They would need little more than a lively fantasy world to indulge their own longing for power. The participants in active political work would doubtless have found confirmation for their proclivities as well. Both could not help but be satisfied with a fiction so thoroughly suited to an ideology of domination.

Chapter 6

'A NEGRO EXCEPTED': RACISM

The ox is the most exasperating animal in the world, a negro excepted.
(Haggard, 1893, 'A Tale of Three Lions')

One final feature of Haggard's writing, the question of race, must now be considered. Although it has been impossible to avoid this issue in the preceding chapters, an attempt at a thorough examination of Haggard's attitude to non-whites now needs to be made. Reserving such an analysis for the final chapter is intended to stress the point that racism, sometimes understood as a cause of imperialism, ought instead to be seen as a consequence, a necessary means of developing and maintaining power, a natural 'conclusion' to Empire.

Racism – the most insidious aspect of British imperialism – was essential to its relative stability. A handy and time-proven agent added for the sustenance of imperialist policies, it functioned as an essential element of British imperial organization. The dictatorial stance of the British towards Africans or Asians could be justified only by racist arguments. Most of these boiled down to two types: either the imperialized peoples were so vastly inferior that they needed enlightened direction or they were so uncivilized that they constituted a threat to the well-being of others, specifically whites, and thus needed enlightened supervision. The determination of one or the other argument seems to have depended on the relative security of the power in control. The matter-of-fact tone of Milner's remarks in a 1901 speech aimed at dramatizing the need for a larger white settlement in South Africa illustrates the way in which the need for white expertise (argument number one) was simply taken for granted:

I am perfectly well aware that the bulk of manual labour in this country must be done, not by white men, but by the coolie and by the Kaffir; but I say that the white population on the land in Natal is greatly insufficient adequately to do, as it ought to be done, even that work which is proper for the white man, and which the white man alone can perform.   (1913, p. 46)

Although the message is clear – whites are needed to do the work that is altogether different from the work done by non-whites – the plainly and indefensibly racist rhetoric is scarcely impassioned or provocative. The more menacing second option, for instance, would probably have appeared more frequently in a period of weak or weakened security. In 1906, when Milner warns the British in his essay 'The Imperialist Creed' that their Empire might well dissolve, he is both more forceful and more intimidating. Governing the 'weaker races' is a political imperative. The colonies, he writes, 'are kept within the Empire solely by the strength of the United Kingdom, by its military and naval power, and by the capacity of its people for the government and administration of weaker races. If that power or that capacity fail us, the dominion is at an end' (1913, p. 264). While the threat of imperial demise is not precisely synonymous with the threat of an onslaught of 'uncivilized' Africans, the idea that the British might one day be unable to govern their so-called racial inferiors by either military or moral means would have been as frightening as it was humiliating.

Imperial-minded writers of fiction and verse were rarely so overt in their use of racist language as the politicians, but their racism was just as pernicious, and it confronted readers of popular fiction in particular with alarming regularity. Much of this literary imperialism reveals a racism by implication, if not by design. Gratuitous insults are scattered at random, set loose by habit, it would seem, rather than by method. Interestingly enough, the gradually developing intensity of racism in literature seems to reflect the historical shift from a relatively self-confident to a more defensive Empire. Stevenson's Indian, Secundra Dass, for example, in *The Master of Ballantrae* (1889), is mainly used for the exoticism and mystery he adds to Ballantrae's character. Paternalism is the word that comes to mind, and it never involves the sort of humiliating interaction between black and white that is found over twenty years later in the early 'Sanders' stories of Edgar Wallace (*Sanders of the River*, 1911; *People of the River*, 1912; and *Bosambo of the River*, 1914). Against a background of lying, sycophancy, and intrigue on the part of the Africans in his district, Sanders, fittingly dressed 'in immaculate white' (Wallace, 1933, p. 190) and tapping his leg suggestively with a switch, affirms the necessity for masterful leadership. Between these quite distinct considerations of race represented by Stevenson and

Edgar Wallace are varying degrees of race consciousness and conflict.

Henty's boy-hero in the viciously banal *With Buller in Natal* (1901), though he regrets the killing of some eighteen Africans during a dynamite attack on a group of Boer supply and ammunition wagons, has little genuine remorse. Indeed, such deaths are not likely to arouse in the reader any more intensely felt regret than that aroused in Henty's character if blacks are scarcely regarded as human. The black servant, Zambo, in Conan Doyle's *The Lost World* is judged to be 'as willing as any horse, and about as intelligent' (1912, p. 94), an estimation that may well have been received at the time as not merely acceptable but even genial. This dehumanization succeeds in placing the non-white outside the bounds of the white reader's sympathy. Surely this is the upshot of David Crawford's remark in Buchan's *Prester John* that Africans are unique because '[t]heir skins are insensitive to pain' (1910, p. 145). 'I have seen a Zulu stand on a piece of red hot iron without noticing it', he says, 'till he was warmed by the smell of burning hide' (1910, p. 145). The Zulu in this case lacked sufficient sensitivity to qualify for even minimal human compassion.

Certain protestations and avowals of a lack of race prejudice are by now easy to discredit. Few would take seriously Dr Jameson's remark that 'Mr Rhodes is absolutely free from contempt for the black man ... [and] looks upon him and treats him as a fellow man, differing simply in his lower level of development' ('Imperialist', 1897, p. 404). But it is not as easy to dismiss C. E. Carrington's observations on Kipling which, despite Carrington's being markedly different from Jameson and having the further advantages of both time and intelligence, are equally short-sighted. Kipling, he circuitously suggests, is relatively free of racial prejudice. Trying to describe what Kipling meant by the White Man's Burden, Carrington explains that, 'In the eighteen-nineties the phrase, "a white man", did not only mean a man with an unpigmented skin; it had a secondary symbolic meaning: a man with the moral standards of the civilized world' (1970, p. 334). One need scarcely ask about the 'secondary symbolic' meaning of 'a black man'. The implications of such 'symbolism' do not appear to trouble Carrington, who proceeds to refine his explanation further:

No one will assert that Rhodes and Kipling and Theodore Roosevelt believed in the political equality of all men, regardless of their social status, as it is asserted today; they would have contemptuously rejected any such notion. It is equally unjust to suppose that they believed in the absolute superiority of certain racial types.   (1970, p. 335)

Whatever the middle ground of their beliefs, their actions and influence were not so difficult to apprehend. Roosevelt, then Governor of New York, sent a letter to Henry Cabot Lodge (12 January 1899) in which he writes, regarding 'The White Man's Burden' Kipling had mailed him, 'I send you an advance copy of a poem by Kipling which is rather poor poetry, but good sense from the expansionist standpoint' (Carrington, 1970, p. 337). The poem was immediately put to good use: it was printed in the London *Times* on 4 February and in the New York *Sun* and *Tribune* on 5 February. The American Senate voted to administer the Philippines on 6 February.

It is not easy to manœuvre with an expression like 'absolute superiority', and Carrington's attempt to do so suggests an element of difficulty in defending his position. We surmise, moreover, that Carrington's personal interest in Kipling has affected his sense of Kipling's disposition towards other races. Even a poem like 'The Mother Lodge', which Carrington suggests as a clue to Kipling's racial attitudes, with its *'Outside – "Sergeant!" Sir! Salute! Salaam!/ Inside – "Brother", an' it doesn't do no 'arm'* (Kipling, 1919, p. 505), offers little besides superficial racial camaraderie and Masonic brotherhood. There is no doubt that the inevitable colliding of racial types appealed to Kipling, to judge from *Kim* (1901) at least. But the notion of the white man's superiority was as firmly fixed in his mind as it was in the minds of others, and it was because of this deep-seated and commonly shared sense of superiority that a phrase like the White Man's Burden could be taken as a metaphor for civilization.

Haggard's Carrington is Alan Sandison, who holds up Haggard as a model of cultural relativism. Sandison's argument goes something like this: since Haggard believed that all people were equally subservient to process and flux, he held all people to be united in such a way that no one could be considered better or worse than anyone else. 'Indeed it is Haggard's presentation of them as being under the same doom as the Europeans and sensitively aware of the fact', Sandison writes, 'that results in the remarkable degree of identification of native and European spiritual life' (1967, p. 31). Everyone, in other words, is equally helpless, equally mortal, and equally subject to the finality and inevitability of death. But for those whose eyes are not constantly straining over the horizon of mortality, and who are set to take in the sights they can understand, Sandison's argument is unimpressive. That Hamlet appreciates that both the beggar and the king are food for worms does not make the prince a democrat. The best evidence of Haggard's racism, of course, is the portrayal of the African in his writings. For Sandison, Haggard's 'presentation of the native African is free on the whole from condescension and disparagement' (1967, p. 33). And so wedded is he to this idea that he can take up a story like 'A Tale of Three Lions', praise Haggard for his clear description of wild animals, and refuse to be bothered by that line from this same story which is quoted at the head of this chapter. In fact, Haggard's intellectual leanings, that is, his spiritualism and fatalism discussed in the foregoing chapters, did not contribute to his supposed cultural relativism but to his very real racism. His fiction and non-fiction alike speak for themselves. Haggard's racism is transparently clear; social antagonisms are built right into his manner of thought.

If racism is an inseparable element of the coherent imperial pattern in Haggard's works, what contradictory evidence might account for confusion on this issue? Surely Sandison sees something in the works to support his own interpretation. In fact, Haggard, like Jameson himself and countless others, was to some extent unaware of the depths of his racial antagonism and periodically affected the pose, however precarious, of an enlightened and fair-minded liberal. The vulnerability of this pose, then, is the first point to establish.

Any idea of unity between black and white in Haggard's fiction is a unity of unequals. Occasional pronouncements to the contrary, however, would seem to contradict this. The first pronouncement to examine occurs in *She*, following Holly's explanation that Amahagger women exist on terms of equality with men. Remarking on this phenomenon with some semblance of open-mindedness, Holly comments rather liberally, it would seem, on the moral implications therein: 'It is very curious to observe how the customs of mankind on this question vary in different countries, making morality an affair of latitude' (1957, p. 94). It is precisely such a pretence at cultural relativism that fires Sandison's argument, but Haggard's willingness to grant a different moral standard – and this willingness itself is never free of condescension – has little to do with his granting of an equal one. More illuminating, perhaps, is the way in which Haggard's so-called cultural relativism figures in his disapproving attitude to missionary work, the very nature of which would bring black and white together. The decision of Umbopa (or Ignosi) to forbid 'praying men' to enter Kukuanaland in *King Solomon's Mines* seems to come, for the most part, from Haggard's anti-missionary feeling. In *The Ghost Kings*, Haggard portrays the missionary Reverend John Dove, known to the Africans as 'the Shouter about Things he does not understand' (1908, p. 30), as a hopelessly unsuccessful proselytizer whose inappropriate behaviour clashes starkly with that of the Africans: 'he quite lacked the sympathetic insight which would enable him to understand that a native with thousands of generations of savagery behind him is a different being from a highly educated Christian, and one who should be judged by another law' (1908, pp. 4–5). Although Allan Quatermain himself is the son of a missionary, he disagrees with his father on the issue of converting Africans to Christianity. All the reader sees of the fruit of his father's work is the Khoisan servant, Hans, whose attempts at piety are absurd. Again, as will become clear, condescension and not tolerance gives shape to this ostensible open-mindedness.

Haggard's disapproval of missionary work seems to have its source in something other than either his own unorthodox religious views or his possible class antagonism to evangelicalism (neither stopped him from supporting the Salvation Army both in England and throughout the 'white' world). Nor does his disapproval stem from concern about alienating Africans from their own culture and society. Surely the African could make a good case against the missionaries, but Haggard objected not to cultural aggression, although he is more willing to comprehend the wrongs of foreign meddling here than in any other area of imperialist intrusion, but to social intercourse between races and cultures. He appears to have thought that the intermingling of blacks and whites bred something grotesque on both sides, each taking on the worst features of the other. His characterization of Frank Müller, the half-English, half-Boer civilian in *Jess*, reveals his general view of the situation. Müller is a man whose lifelong contact with Africans has, according to Haggard, divested him of the virtues of both civilized and savage societies:

Too civilized to possess those savage virtues which . . . represent the quantum of innate good nature has thought fit to allow in the mixture, Man; and too barbarous to be subject to the tenderer restraints of cultivated society, he is at once strong in the strength of both and weak in their weaknesses. Animated by the spirit of barbarism, superstition; and almost entirely destitute of the spirit of civilization, mercy, he stands on the edge of both, as terrific a moral spectacle as the world can afford. (1889a, p. 200)

Frank Müller is a typical example of what may happen 'in those places where a handful of a superior race rule over the dense thousands of an inferior' (1889a, p. 199). Without the moral pressure that is exerted by a large number of one's peers, one is, as it were, 'without the law'. One's comparative isolation contributes to a highly marked individuality that could not survive in 'civilized' society. A white person who gets too close to Africans runs the risk of gradual deterioration. In *The Ghost Kings*, Ishmael, who has actually taken African wives, is described as 'probably only one of those broken soldiers of fortune of whom she [Rachel Dove] had met several, who took to the wilderness as a last resource, and by degrees sank to the level of the savages among whom they lived, a person who was not worth a second thought' (1908, p. 38). For Haggard, a white person always reaches the level of an African by 'sinking'; there is no horizontal movement. It is this sinking process which is implied in Andrew Lang's dedication to Haggard in *The Wrong Paradise* (1886): 'We are all savages under our white skins; but you alone recall to us the delights and terrors of the world's nonage.' The African is the common denominator in humankind, the primitive, savage state. Clearly, then, Haggard's statement that morality is an affair of latitude must be understood in this context.

Remarks carrying an aura of liberal tolerance are made with some regularity by either Quatermain or some variation of the Quatermain type. An observer of cultural phenomena and human nature, Quatermain sees himself as a student of the 'history, religions, customs, and habits of the inhabitants of southern, eastern and South Central Africa' (1926b, p. 1). At the beginning of *Allan Quatermain*, the enervating effects of English society lead Quatermain to expatiate upon the meaning of civilization in a passage that at the same time proclaims and belies his cultural relativism:

Ah! this civilisation, what does it all come to? Full forty years and more I spent among savages, and studied them and their nature; and now for several years I have lived here in England, and in my own stupid manner have done my best to learn the ways of the children of light; and what do I find? A great gulf fixed? No, only a very little one, that a plain man's thought may spring across. I say that as the savage is, so is the white man, only the latter is more inventive, and possesses a faculty of combination; save and except also that the savage, as I have known him, is to a large extent free from the greed of money, which eats like a cancer into the heart of the white man. It is a depressing conclusion, but in all essentials the savage and the child of civilisation are identical . . . Civilisation is only savagery silver-gilt.

(1919a, pp. 12–13)

To those readers familiar with the Quatermain stories and the patronizing way in which Quatermain generally interacts with black characters, this rhetoric sounds especially hollow. Moreover, the African's supposed lack of a faculty of combination and inferior inventive powers are hardly the meagre insufficiencies that Quatermain suggests they are. They just happen to separate the human from the animal species. The points of similarity between the 'child of civilization' and the 'savage' are precisely what Quatermain finds depressing.

And what are those 'essentials' that make up this similarity anyway? They are basic emotional responses to experience, enumerated by Quatermain as 'passions, hopes, fears, joys, aspirations towards good and evil and what not' (Haggard, 1919a, p. 14), this last being symptomatic of the almost sedulous imprecision which distinguishes the Quatermain voice. These 'essentials' go to make up what Haggard chooses to call 'human nature', on which subject he, or at least Quatermain, considers himself an expert. Not surprisingly, Haggard's concept of 'human nature' is basically restrictive, defining humanity by its severe limitations. Quatermain justifies his digression on civilization in *Allan Quatermain* by pointing to its usefulness in heightening our awareness of human nature and its bounds:

It seems to me indeed very desirable that we should sometimes try to understand our limitations, so that we may not be carried away by the pride of knowledge. Man's cleverness is almost infinite, and stretches like an elastic band, but human nature is like an iron ring. You can go round and round it, you can polish it highly, you can even flatten it a little on one side, whereby you will make it bulge out upon the other, but you will *never*, while the world endures and man is man, increase its total circumference. It is the one fixed unchangeable thing – fixed as the stars, more enduring than the mountains, unalterable as the way of the Eternal. (1919a, p. 14)

Few formulations are more convenient than that of human nature. Innate and fixed, it is a ready abstraction used to convince us of our limitations, to confine us willingly to the boundaries we know, and to prevent us from crossing to those that are unexplored. Not only, then, are all people equal by dint of their subjection to the design of fate; they are also equal by dint of their subjection to their changeless nature. It is in a society that is, by western standards, relatively undeveloped that Haggard finds evidence to support such ideas. The immutable 'truths' of life which he sees in this society obscure its reality by veiling objective and substantially political differences with subjective philosophical abstractions. The result is a distorted vision of Empire which precludes the possibility of distinguishing between, for one thing, the fears of a subject people and the fears of its ruler. With pseudo-anthropological gusto, Haggard views the African black with an eye to uncovering the fundamental nature of all people. But can one understand the basic elements of life by examining a people subject to a foreign power? Can one endorse this notion of a universal human nature without making too little of the fact that whites ruled and blacks served, whites employed and blacks were employed, and whites were educated and skilled and blacks uneducated and unskilled? The surface coating of silver which, for Haggard, differentiates white from black society is thus far more valuable than he would have us believe.

Whatever Haggard meant by his insistence on the similarities between white and black it had little to do with national or political rights and freedoms. From the very first essays that he wrote in the Transvaal, to his history of the Zulu War, *Cetywayo*, and on through his fiction, speeches, and private diaries, Haggard's political views remained consistently racist. The early essays from the Transvaal show him as paternalistic at best. In 'The Transvaal' (1877), Haggard characterizes the British as uniquely able to rule black Africans with a measure of justice: 'We alone of all the nations in the world know how to control coloured races without the exercise of cruelty' (1877b, p. 78). He does not pretend to believe, however, that British rule will lead to the development necessary for anything like free and independent statehood, and in 'A Zulu War Dance' (1877), which appeared two months after 'The Transvaal', he concedes the chance of there being insufficient potential in blacks to advance to the level of their white rulers:

Civilization, it would seem, when applied to black races, produces effects dramatically opposite to those we are accustomed to observe in white nations; it debases before it can elevate; and as regards the Kafirs it is doubtful, and remains to be proved, whether it has much power to elevate them at all.

(1877a, p. 96)

That British rule was debasing is undeniable; but the implication of this passage is that the elements involved in this debasement were to be found in the blacks themselves. People need more than the basics of human nature, then, to be truly civilized.

In the fiction, racism appears primarily in the shape of indirect slurs, the wanton use of the black for 'dramatic' effect, abysmally unhumorous comic relief, and vapid characterization. That some people felt his portrayal of the black to be thoroughly convincing should not go unnoticed. A contemporary reviewer of *Joan Haste* (1895), who objects to Haggard's unsubtle rendering of the English characters in the book, is delighted with his skill 'in reading the clear-marked lines of savage natures' ('Novel notes', November 1895, p. 229). As late as 1972 this oversimplified image of the African receives disturbingly appreciative praise. A Canadian doctoral dissertation on Haggard describes one of the servants in *Jess* as 'an early example of the author's sympathy for and understanding of the African native. Childlike, timid, shrewd, superstitious, sulky and unreliable, but extremely lovable, Jantjé has an unmistakable air of reality' (Bursey, 1972, p. 16). Even now, it seems, the point must still be made that crude and simplistic characters offer little more than proof of the necessity of imperial control. If the merry and witless African was no product of painstaking characterization, he was also no accident of history.

Haggard's romances are so replete with casually dispensed and dismissive slurs and indignities that racism is more a given of the African scene than a preached doctrine. Like Haggard himself, his white characters advance themselves as great friends of the blacks at the same time as their behaviour consistently belies their assertions. In *The People of the Mist*, Leonard Outram is convinced that his servant, Otter, is his best friend, but he remains content to have his best friend serve at his table. Quatermain, likewise, persists in attacking Boer bigotry while seemingly unaware of his own prejudices. In *Marie*, one of Haggard's most generous descriptions of Boer life, Quatermain condemns the race prejudice of the Boers on one page and refers to the 'stinking savage' African on the next. An absurd irony is this combination of asserted tolerance and practised racism, but it offers some explanation of how imperialists justified their exploitative system.

To a contemporary reader, it is Haggard's dehumanization of the African that is especially noticeable. The faultless Rachel Dove recollects her childhood in *The Ghost Kings* and remembers when she at least had Boer children to play with who were 'white and human' (1908, p. 7). In *Allan Quatermain*, it is the fair-haired, idle, and imperious Flossie Mackenzie, who makes her contempt for Africans clear. So pleased that 'every native for miles round . . . is ready to do what [she] want[s]' (1919a, p. 57) that she claims not to miss the advantages of a European upbringing, Flossie is kidnapped by and (all too soon) saved from the Masai, who dare to examine her hair and white skin 'with their filthy paws' (1919a, p. 107). Even Quatermain's admiration for Umslopogaas is undercut by Haggard's dehumanization. In *Allan Quatermain*, the two 'friends' are hurriedly riding back to Milosis from a battle outside the city when one of their horses gives out and Umslopogaas decides to run on foot for the rest of the way. Quatermain is thus given the opportunity to admire Umslopogaas's tremendous physical power and stamina: 'It was a wonderful thing to see old Umslopogaas run mile after mile, his lips slightly parted and his nostrils agape like the horse's' (1919a, p. 284). Such objectivity and indifference to Umslopogaas's discomfort, partly the result of Quatermain's proprietary attitude to the black warrior, also allows for the gratingly nuanced distinctions in Quatermain's announcement of their presence at the gates of Milosis after the monumental race is over: 'It is the Lord Macumazahn, and with him is his dog, his black dog' (1919a, p. 285). Clearly the image of the African in this context – mere animal, if heroic – does little to emphasize the similarity between white and black.

The majority of the Africans in the fiction, it should be said, do not hold the centre stage as Umslopogaas does. Instead, they fill out the sometimes rather elaborate African settings. This background effect is one reason why so much of the racism in Haggard's fiction may be perceived as a diffusion of minor details – the scarcely noted absence of a litter or bed, a greeting or acknowledgement – although the passing and piecemeal slights build, by accumulation, a definite code of behaviour. This exotic landscape effect also moderates still another aspect of Haggard's racism, that of the expendability of the African, the indifferent slaughtering of any number of blacks for an exciting scene. Much of the adventure – also brutality and gore – of the fiction is achieved at the expense of the black. The excitement of the elephant hunt in *King Solomon's Mines*, for instance, comes when Khiva, a Zulu boy, is seized by an elephant that tears him in two and then collapses upon his remains after being shot. Other sensational mutilations are made possible by the seemingly endless flow of black victims; whites seem magically immune to such disasters. In *Allan Quatermain*, Quatermain hacks off the hand of a Masai warrior in the middle of the night, leaving us with the lurid image of a black hand clutching a knife buried deep in the chest of Quatermain's servant. Later on in the book, a freshly severed human head that further excites the reader is that of the missionary Mackenzie's servant. This last sight prompts the missionary to remark gratefully that, ' "It is the head of one of the men who accompanied Flossie. . . Thank God it is not hers!" ' (1919a, p. 70). The loss of a black, either through accident or in battle, is only momentarily regrettable; it is certainly not an occasion for this man of God to grieve. The action of the story can proceed just as vigorously as before. In *Marie*, blacks are literally not even counted in the numbering of casualties and deaths. Upon finding the surviving members of some trek Boers whose disastrous attempt to migrate to Delagoa Bay ended in starvation, death, and misery, Quatermain remarks: 'Of the original thirty-five souls, not reckoning natives, who had accompanied Henri Marais upon his ill-fated expedition, there now remained but nine' (1912, p. 128). Individual African lives are either dispensable or invisible.

A lack of individuality in the character of the African, the result of insufficiencies in the matters of both respect and intimacy, allows Haggard to use the black not only for sensational adventure, but also for blatantly racist comic relief. Helping to form the stereotypic mould of the comic black figure that became standard fare in the popular literature and films of the first half of this century, Haggard places his fictional blacks, mostly servants, in obsequious and demeaning postures in order for them to serve as clowns or buffoons. Hans, the Khoisan Christian convert who appears in many of the Quatermain adventures, is the best example of this use of the stereotypically tractable African character as an instrument of humour. It is clear that when Haggard trots out Hans to be humiliated, kicked, and scorned, it is for fun. Hans is predictably simple-minded and irresponsible, playing the fool to Quatermain in exchange for the most minor of favours. He is totally at Quatermain's mercy for even so small a thing as tobacco, and this dependency forces uncomfortably farcical situations which display his fatuous, blundering and often unsuccessful attempts to satisfy his needs, exploiting the full misery of the situation. Meekly sucking on an empty pipe and thus indicating that he would like Quatermain to fill it, Hans approaches the latter, Haggard writes, 'much as a dog groans heavily under the table when he wants a bit to eat' (1921, p. 103). After receiving some of the wished-for tobacco with humble thanks, he 'wriggle[s] away like a worm' (1921, p. 105) under Quatermain's observant eye.

If Quatermain is the invincible English hero, Hans is his unheroic antithesis. Quatermain's faithful servant is a man with pitiable weaknesses of the flesh, the greatest of these being his love of drink. In *Treasure of the Lake*, Hans's desire for gin and his indulgence in palm-wine give Quatermain the opportunity to throw a stool at him so that Hans must run away only to return even more abjectly later on. Of course, Hans is not simply a buffoon. He is also, as Quatermain insists, his master's old friend, 'in his own way' (1926b, p. 22). But such friendship falls very short of the mark, and it is during their friendly interaction, in conversations heavily punctuated with 'Yes, Baas!' 'Very good, Baas!' 'Oh, Baas', or some slight variation of the same, that one gets some glimpse of its vast inadequacy.

Although *Nada the Lily* does not counterbalance the negative aspects of Haggard's other fiction, it stands out, along with the Zulu trilogy *Marie*, *Child of Storm*, and *Finished*, as a book that is largely free of racist ideology. Because it focuses exclusively on black society, ideas of racial supremacy do not obtrude in the story, and the reader is considerably less conscious of matters of race than in other works. Even the narrator of the tale, Mopo, father of Nada, putative father of Umslopogaas, and murderer of the unconscionable Shaka, is black, and this seems to affect, to some advantage, both the tone and the telling of the story. To begin with, Mopo indulges in much less philosophizing than characters in other works, and without these irritating philosophical passages, the reader can settle down to enjoy the adventure itself, with its nice twists of plot and its generally convincing sense of history. In addition, Mopo is clearly the result of a fair effort on Haggard's part to capture the style of traditional

African tale-telling as he himself may have heard it. For once, Haggard seems convincingly close to his African source. The absence of white characters (there is one listening to Mopo tell his story) frees Haggard from the obligatory setting up of awkward relations between races and allows him to chronicle an unusually interesting historical adventure.

Several scenes in *Nada* have tremendous power; whole sections are impressively strange and characteristic of Haggard's creative vigour in top form. Shaka's elaborate and demonic ritual of mourning for his dead mother, whom he has killed himself, by forcing his people to cry for days until they kill each other in frustration and misery, is full of that unadulterated malevolence often found in traditional romantic villainy.[1] Haggard's imagination seems to be at its best again in the creation of the character Galazi, the wild Wolf Boy who lives with the wolves of Ghost Mountain. Kipling credits a description of wolves in *Nada* as the inspiration for his own wolf stories (Cohen, 1968, pp. 31–2). Further, Haggard creates a mythology in *Nada* to which most readers, but children in particular, would be responsive: the People of the Axe, the stories of Ghost Mountain, the legend of the woman Nada, and the quasi-magical weapons – Groan-Maker, the Axe, and Watcher of Fords – are especially appealing.

Certain features of Haggard's fiction that are usually irritating in the extreme are here quite in keeping with the rest of the book. Even when Mopo begins a familiar Haggardian discourse on the meaning of life, it seems to suit the character of a very old man who has survived the leadership of Shaka, Dingane, and Mpande, seen an inordinate amount of misery, and is waiting for death. Secondly, one does not feel that the cruelty he attributes to Shaka and Dingane, cruelty that borders narrowly on sadism (Dingane sends his impis into a fire to prove little else but his power to do so), is the typically excessive indulgence in blood and gore that typifies other Haggard adventures, for these Zulu kings were not known for their virtues of mercy and pity.[2] Finally, even when Mopo, in typical Quatermain fashion, says that he cannot describe the slaughter he has seen, it seems genuine incapacity on the part of the character rather than unremitting incompetence on the part of the author. Mopo is so truly agonized by the memory that it does indeed seem unspeakable.

Notwithstanding these positive points, *Nada* is still clumsily flawed by Haggard's racial consciousness. Nada, the legendary Helen-like beauty who brings death to all who love her, is given a white woman's features as if to account for her well-favoured appearance. Not only does she have a light complexion and hair that is not as tightly curled as the hair of other Zulu women, but she may have some white blood as well to explain her singular beauty. Mopo explains that although his wife was the child of a Swazi woman, the man in whose house she was raised may not have been her father. She was born at a time when a Portuguese man was staying with her tribe, and it was rumoured that he had fathered the child. Mopo himself admits to not knowing the truth of these rumours: 'I only speak of them because the beauty of Nada was rather as is the beauty of the white people than of ours, and this might happen if her grandfather chanced to be a white man' (1892a, p. 47). Another weakness in *Nada* is the strained and often bombastic language of Haggard's Africans. Haggard seems to be attempting an English re-creation of vernacular Zulu, in particular the kind of ceremonial diction used by the practitioners of traditional oral folklore. For the most part, his efforts fail. However noble and heroic the African characters are meant to be, their ponderous speech is often ineffective. In response to exactly this sort of problem, H. F. Ellis in 1959 playfully remarks that Haggard 'might have told us where he got the idea that Zulu chieftains and High Priests and Queens of Zu-Vendis speak, and should be addressed, in the prose of the Authorized Version. "Dost" and "hast" and "peradventure" are meat and drink to them' (p. 78). Ellis goes so far as to suggest that Haggard may well have invented a convention that was later used in popular fictional adventures for 'any un-English types ... whose normal speech would tend to be unintelligible. In his own interests he should have fathered the idea on somebody else' (1959, p. 78).

Outside the fiction, Haggard is most voluble on the subject of blacks in *Cetywayo*, and once again he exhibits the same kind of self-righteous and deluded racial thinking found in the African romances. In the following passage, which appears during a discussion of the Boers' plan to occupy Zulu territory, his ostensible attack on the idea of racial superiority quickly dissolves into paternalistic racism:

This plan was supported by arguments about the superiority of the white races and their obvious destiny to rule. It is, I confess, one that I look upon as little short of wicked. I could never discover a superiority *so great* in ourselves as to authorise us, by right divine as it were, to destroy the coloured man and take his land ... Of course there is another extreme. Nothing is more ridiculous than the length to which the black brother theory is sometimes driven by enthusiasts. A savage is one thing and a civilised man is another; and though civilised men may and do become savages, I personally doubt if the converse is even possible. But whether the civilised man, with his gun, his greed, and his dynamite, is really so very superior to the savage is another question, and one which would bear argument . . . My point is, that his superiority is not at any rate so absolutely overwhelming as to justify him in the wholesale destruction of the savage, and the occupation of his lands.   (1896, p. liii)

While seemingly at odds with the Boers, he differs with them only in a matter of degree: the superiority of white people is merely not as great as the Boers believe. The target of Haggard's attack, in fact, is not the arbitrary authority of white over black but the potentially catastrophic results he expected would follow Boer rule. White superiority remains intact. Gin, greed, and dynamite admittedly bring it down a few pegs on the racial scale, but the scale is none the less operative. What is most telling about this passage, however, is the familiar suggestion that whereas whites can go so far as to sink to the level of the African, the African can probably never rise to the level of civilized white society.

On the condition that a just and equitable government be made available to the blacks (that is, British, not Boer administration), Haggard gives his sanction to white rule. Indeed, it is in the realm of proper rule that he holds out most hope for change in the African. In the following passage, also from *Cetywayo*, he reiterates his disapproval of any policy that would lead to the devastation of the African people and affirms the potency of 'just government':

I cannot believe that the Almighty, who made both white and black, gave to one race the right or mission of exterminating or even of robbing or maltreating the other, and calling the process the advance of civilisation. It seems to me, that on only one condition, if at all, have we the right to take the black man's land; and that is, that we . . . allow no maltreatment of them, either as individuals or tribes, but on the contrary, do our best to elevate them, and wean them from savage customs. Otherwise the practice is surely indefensible.   (1896, p. 270)

By savage customs Haggard means those he specifically cited in *King Solomon's Mines* – the corrupt practices of diviners and the sentencing of people to death without trial – as well as polygamy and chieftainship. But he offers no evidence of faith in a future where the two races would stand on an equal footing.

146

Reflecting the change from arrogant paternalism to the harsher racism of post-Boer War days, Haggard shows an increasing apprehensiveness about the potential strength of the non-white world in a 1905 speech to the Canadian Club in Ottawa. Interestingly enough, he shifts his gaze from Africa to Japan and China and begins to display signs of a racially linked xenophobia that increases in its intensity until the end of his life. Turning a discussion on land reform into a bitter tirade on the tendency for people to migrate to the cities, Haggard is quick to point out that the effects of city-living on the birth rate of white nations could be disastrous. Cities, he reasons, do not breed a sufficient number of white children to permit a nation to carry on at full strength:

> on the land alone will the supply of children be available that is necessary to carry on our white races. And if they are not carried on in sufficient numbers what of it? Of course, you have all heard of what they call the yellow peril, and many people have laughed at it as a bogey. Is it a bogey? Does Russia, for instance, consider that Japan is a mere nightmare? I think not.
>
> (1926a, II, p. 268)

China is perceived as equally threatening. If the Chinese decide they need land, and they see 'an island continent half vacant and other places with a few families scattered over the land, and a few millions heaped together in the things these white people call cities' (1926, II, p. 269), they will take the land and nothing will stop them. They will have the strength of their enormous population. After assuring his Canadian friends that this nightmare may become all too real, and that it may endanger not only Britain but their own country as well, Haggard urges them to boost the white population of Canada with British immigrants:

> Now, gentlemen, how does this apply to the very great country in which I am today? . . . I say that very soon there is going to be enormous competition for immigration, for population, and especially for Anglo-Saxons; that the time is coming when these people will be bid for, when they will be sought for, when they will be paid for – paid any price to get them. And I venture to say to you: Get them while you can, get them from home, get them from England.
>
> (1926a, II, p. 270)

Surely these are not the sentiments of a man who has escaped the vice of racial prejudice.

By 1913 Haggard was predicting that future political struggles in South Africa would not involve a clash between 'Briton and Boer', but between white and black, an opinion he held for the rest of his life. Assessing the situation between the British and the Boers in a letter to *The Times*, he states: 'To my mind the great question of the future in Southern Africa is not, as so many suppose, that of the political dominance of Englishman or Boer, but of the inevitable, though let us hope, far-off struggle for practical supremacy between the white blood and the black' (16 August 1913, p. 5). Eleven years later, Haggard envisages this conflict between white and black as being one of global concern, and not limited merely to South Africa. In his diary of 9 August 1924, he records: 'The great ultimate war, as I have always held, will be that between the white and the coloured races' (XXII, p. 123). In September of the same year, after seeing a census report on South Africa, Haggard continues to express concern about the fate of its white population: 'In short if South Africa does not wish to "go black", it had better inaugurate a very energetic immigration policy, which up to the present it has entirely declined to do' (29 September 1924, XXII, p. 181). Haggard's war-time work for the Royal Colonial Institute, which involved travelling to South Africa, Australia, and Canada in order to help settle ex-British servicemen in the Dominions, was for him intended to initiate a whites-only immigration policy that would protect the Empire and certainly forestall the eventuality of South Africa's 'going black'. He says as much in a letter to *The Times*:

Always it has been my conviction that the future safety and greatness of the British Empire depended upon the redistribution of Empire population of white blood. Indeed, as such bodies as the Royal Colonial Institute and the Salvation Army can bear witness, directly or indirectly, I have given a good many years of my life, together with the best of such energies as I possess to attempt to advance this great end. (31 March 1922, p. 8)

This from a man who sincerely felt himself to be a friend to the blacks of Africa.

To accuse Haggard, who probably knew more about and had more sympathy for African society than most of his contemporaries, of having been a racist is to grant that he was very much a man of his time and his class. A man of Haggard's stamp is not often in the forefront of liberalism. His African experience exercised an addition-

148

ally persuasive conservative force. Seeing Haggard's racism in its entirety, then, means seeing it as a significant part of the British body politic. It means seeing the way a particular pattern of imperialist thought adapted to the post-war international scene. Throughout his pre-war life, Haggard's nationalism, vulgar heroism, and authoritarianism were never far from anti-semitism, xenophobia, and other reactionary sentiments. Following the war, however, these views combined with his vehement anti-trade unionism and anti-Bolshevism, among other aversions, to yield a frighteningly proto-fascist mentality. Haggard gives us only a glimpse of what others of like mind went on to become.

In the pre-war fiction, anti-semitism is a banal commonplace. Rapacious Jews exploit the misfortunes of bona fide gentlemen in *The People of the Mist.* Jews are hook-nosed, fierce-eyed Christ killers in *She* and *The World's Desire.* Their money cannot disguise their foulness: Jewish women may be drenched in diamonds but they betray themselves with their dirty fingernails in *Dawn.* The attention to unlovely detail is as important here as in the characterization of the African, and it is expressive of a deep-seated repugnance. During the First World War, these fictional prejudices fed into Haggard's obsessive fear of communism. In Haggard's diaries, to which he committed his thoughts during the war and then for the rest of his life, we see a man for whom not only Jews, communists, and trade unionists, but also Irish, Quebecois, and Indian nationalists all spelled trouble. (It is unfortunate that D. S. Higgins, editor of *The Private Diaries of Sir Henry Rider Haggard*, chose to omit the worst of this material in his selection.) By far, it is the Jews and the communists who are the targets of most of Haggard's venom at this time. Some of his diary entries are horrifying, but they also seem undeniably of a piece with his earlier imperialist views.

It is clear that the Russian Revolution positively haunted Haggard. (He served as president of the short-lived Liberty League, an organization formed, as he states in a letter to *The Times,* 'to combat the advance of Bolshevism in the United Kingdom and throughout the Empire' [3 March 1920, p. 12].) He was almost equally concerned about the state of post-war Europe. In the diaries, Jews were blamed for both. Bolshevism in England was simply a 'great Jewish plot' (14 August 1920, XV, p. 182). On 14 August 1920, Haggard recorded that both British Labour leaders and communists were victims of this ruinous Jewish conspiracy:

But behind these Labour leaders, although they may not know it, behind even the ordinary vapouring Communist, stands the sinister figure of the Jew, the Jew who desires to destroy civilization in order that like a new Colossus he may bestride its ruins and rake the earth of wealth, wherewith he would build his new empire. Out of 22 Members of Council of Commissaries of the Soviet Government 17 are Jews, all the department of the Interior and most of the War Department are Jews: Trotztsky or Bronstein, the high priest of the new faith is a Jew – and so forth. Further all these happenings from the commencement of the Russian Revolution on exactly follow the lines laid down in the 'Jewish Peril'. (XV, p. 183)

On 18 August 1920 he reiterates this tedious anti-semitic line that Jews controlled the Russian Revolution: 'Strange as it may seem all this Russian trouble is caused by a handful of vile Jews and agitators' (XV, p. 191). In his entry for the following day, Haggard claims that Jews are also a significant threat to the Empire, *The Daily Herald* being 'practically a Bolshevist organ largely financed by foreign Jews, whose announced object is the destruction of the British Empire' (19 August 1920, XV, p. 191). On the same day and on 23 August, Haggard blames the murder of the Romanovs on Jews as well and reminds himself that, after all, Jews were Christ killers too (19, 23 August 1920, XV, pp. 191, 195, 203). Five days later, on 28 August, Haggard confides the following to his diary, again regarding the death of the Romanovs: 'The tendency of the Jew to torture before he kills is a curious indication of his character which apparently has not varied since the days of Pontius Pilate' (XV, p. 218). Haggard sums up the situation in Russia simply and concisely on 6 December 1921: 'In short Russia is a hell where a few Jews and other devils have obtained the mastery over millions, who no longer have the courage to band together and defend themselves' (XVIII, p. 77).

Throughout the early twenties the diaries are sprinkled with more of the same. Haggard notes with alarm on 14 January 1921 the tremendous rate of Jewish immigration into the United States: 'The States at the moment are being swamped by immigrants, an enormous proportion of whom are Jews from Central Europe, and does not know how to stem the torrent, although it desires to have no more jews in the country where the native americans are vanishing under a flood of aliens' (XVI, p. 177). Two years later (24 January 1923) Jews are alleged to have been involved in some Christian travesties performed in Moscow during the 1922 Christmas season (XX, pp. 125–6). Jews were also at fault, according to his 1923 diary entry, for the awful state of affairs in Germany. All Germans must undergo terrible suffering except for 'the "magnates" and the horrible Teutonic Jews who sit like spiders in Berlin, Vienna and elsewhere, and suck out the life-blood of the unhappy peoples that they have got into their net' (27 August 1923, XXI, p. 67).

In April of 1924 we see the direction that Haggard might have taken had he lived long enough when he writes, regarding the labour situation in England, 'Must England collapse or will it ever find a Mussolini?' (30 April 1924, XXII, p. 30). Mussolini comes in for more praise on 1 September 1924 as Haggard notes approvingly that he has 'driven the Bolshevist and Communist swine into the sea' (XXII, p. 154). On 6 January 1925, Haggard once more speaks on Mussolini's behalf:

Mussolini is face to face with the crisis and, as usual, is taking strong measures in the Italian Chambers. Personally I believe that he will win against the Liberals or the Socialists and hope that this may be the case. Whatever his faults and extravagances he has dragged Italy out of the Communistic mire and set her upon her feet again. (XXII, p. 260)

Haggard's attitude to pre-fascist Germany is equally revealing. On 16 August 1923, Haggard's diary entry indicates that he accepted uncritically and indifferently not only the reports but also the sentiments of his nephew-in-law, Artic Charlton, then Consul General in Berlin, regarding anti-Jewish outbreaks of violence:

the profiteers, especially the Jew profiteers, flaunt their wealth before them [the German people]. There have, it is true, been occasional outbreaks which may always be foretold by the sudden disappearance of the Jews who somehow seem to know when they are coming and bolt for their holes like rats until the trouble is over. This soon happens for even such indignation or starvation movements in Germany must be organized and directed from above and the moment such pressure ceases, they cease also, because the German cannot act on his own initiative. (XXII, p. 130)

One wonders what Haggard would have said when the organization of anti-semitic activity was subsequently 'directed from above' with such infernal success. Ironically, Haggard's anti-semitism prevented him from seeing the possibility of a Jewish political state. He argues cynically that Jews would not settle in Palestine 'in great numbers . . . for in Jerusalem there is little money to be made' (26 April 1920, XV, p. 50). Fortunately he was equally wrong about many other things as well.

CONCLUSION

Rider Haggard was an imperial propagandist, a man who made use of every opportunity to advance matters relating to Empire. In 1920, just five years before his death, Haggard sent a letter to *The Times* in which, with characteristically naive immodesty, he called attention to his long years of devotion to the imperial cause. 'All my life', he wrote, 'so far as opportunity was open to me, by means of fictional and other writings, and as a humble servant of the country, I have done my best to spread knowledge of the Empire and all it means or should mean to us' (7 February 1920, p. 8). Similarly, *The Days of My Life* ends with Haggard's description of himself as 'most of all, perhaps, a lover of his country, which, with heart and soul and strength, he has tried to serve to the best of his small powers and opportunities' (1926a, II, p. 232). With its imaginative renderings of African people, geography, and history, his fiction gave the Empire a semblance of reality to the British at home. In the works in which Haggard makes use of his knowledge of both legend and historical facts, there are accounts of the Great Trek of the Boers, the first Boer War, the Zulu War, and the rise and fall of the Zulu nation. In the more fantastical of the romances there are implicit allusions to Empire, some of which emerge in passing, others informing the whole. Even in works that have predominantly English settings, an officer just returned from the war, a son lost in the Boer War, or an imperial speech made in Parliament stand as reminders of the Empire. Through his fiction, the ideas and attitudes that accrue to imperialism were conveyed almost effortlessly to the largely uncritical and accepting reader. Ideas and attitudes not easily taken in as huge hunks of political theory were readily assimilated as opinions and biases. As a public servant Haggard was probably greatly underrated. His fiction, only superficially innocuous, contributed generously to the process of shaping the imperial mentality.

Haggard's writings are far more than mere literary-historical arte-

153

facts, although even at that they would still be of interest. What allows them to transcend the moment of their time is the precise nature of the link to their historical era, since Haggard's popular and accessible style, which incorporates his questionable and potentially dangerous ideas and ideals, will undoubtedly repeat itself, with variations, in the works of other writers. An examination of the relationship between literature and propaganda is thus always instructive. Who are the heroes of a particular literary work, we must ask, and what do they stand for? What are the reasons for the things they do? It is essential to pay close attention to the sort of soft propaganda, like Haggard's, that secures interest in the shape of historical romance, fantasy, adventure, or thrillers, and effectively checks one's critical abilities. Such literature, with its excessive dependence on watchwords and formulas, its sanctioned prejudices and antipathies, goes a long way towards fostering a limited moral consciousness. Haggard's writing, which certainly contributed to the failure of consciousness in his own time, shows the manner in which literature can work to inhibit a reader's essential critical and hence moral power. Coming to terms with its ideological force is perhaps a small way of protecting that power from a similar fate today.

NOTES

---

1. The days of his life

1. Rider Haggard, *Cetywayo and His White Neighbours*, 2nd edn (1882; London: Kegan Paul, Trench, Trübner, and Co., 1896), pp. 25–6; R. C. K. Ensor, *England, 1870–1914* (Oxford University Press, 1936), p. 58. A good sense of what Haggard knew about events in the Transvaal, Natal, and Zululand may be gained from *Cetywayo*. Other historians, for example, Joseph Lehmann in *The First Boer War* (London: Jonathan Cape, 1972), Eric A. Walker in his standard *A History of Southern Africa*, 3rd edn (London: Longmans, 1965), Oliver Ransford in *The Battle of Majuba Hill* (London: John Murray, 1967), and Donald R. Morris in *The Washing of the Spears* (London: Jonathan Cape, 1966), refer to Haggard in their books. I have cited *Cetywayo* when it appears to be as accurate as later accounts of the subject, but have used other sources when necessary. *Cetywayo* must clearly be supplemented by less partisan studies which give fuller details of such matters as the abrogation of Boer rights by the British. Lehmann and Ransford's books are especially helpful in illuminating the particular events experienced by Haggard.

2. See George Saintsbury, review of *The Witch's Head*, *Academy*, XXVII (17 January 1885), 41; unsigned reviews in *Saturday Review*, LIX (17 January 1885), 84–5; *Athenaeum*, LXXXV (10 January 1850), 49; and *Literary World* (London), XXXI, N.S. (6 February 1885), 130–1.

3. John Hobson's remarks on the protective tariff issue in *Imperialism*, rev. edn (1902; Ann Arbor: University of Michigan Press, 1965) suggest that it is possible to group Haggard with others who claim not to believe in protection but support it implicitly. Hobson says that 'the most formidable mask of Protection will take the shape of military necessity. A military nation surrounded by hostile empires must have within her boundaries adequate supplies of the sinews of war, efficient recruits, and a large food supply. We cannot safely rely upon the fighting capacity of a town-bred population, or upon food supplies from foreign lands. Both needs demand that checks be set upon the excessive concentration of our population in towns, and that a serious attempt be made to revive agriculture and restore the people to the soil' (p. 103).

155

2. The politics of romance

1. Haggard has this to say about war in *The Days of My Life*: 'However painful the fact, it remains true that man is a fighting animal, and from the time of Homer down, and probably for tens of thousands of years before it, some of his finest qualities – such as patriotism, courage, obedience to authority, patience in disaster, fidelity to friends and a noble cause, endurance, and so forth – have been evolved in the exercise of war' (London: Longmans, Green, 1926a), I, pp. 103–4.

2. There is an obvious parallel between *Queen Sheba's Ring* and Kipling's poem 'The Islanders' (1902). The Islanders are like the Abati, smug, isolated, indifferent to military duty but not to their leisure, people with a great historic legacy but no immediate strength. Kipling's bitter criticism is reminiscent of Haggard's:

> Fenced by your careful fathers, ringed by your leaden seas,
> Long did ye wake in quiet and long lie down at ease;
> Till ye said of Strife, 'What is it?' Of the Sword,
> > 'It is far from our ken;'
> Till ye made a sport of your shrunken hosts and a toy of your
> > armed men.
> > Ye stopped your ears to the warning – Ye would neither look
> > nor heed –
> > Ye set your leisure before their toil and your lusts above their
> > need.

(*Kipling's Verse*, New York: Doubleday, Page, 1919, pp. 347–8)

3. Kipling's story 'The Comprehension of Private Copper', in *Traffics and Discoveries* (Toronto: Morang and Company, 1904), is strikingly similar to *Jess*. Briefly, Private Copper meets an English renegade during the Boer War and is told that 'England sent an English gentleman [Wolseley], who could not tell a lie, to say that so long as the sun rose and the rivers ran in their courses the Transvaal would belong to England' (pp. 150–1). The renegade's father had been a shopkeeper, 'In those days [when] one used to believe in the British Government' (p. 151). When 'the Transvaal wiped the earth with the English' (p. 151) and England did nothing to save the colonials, the renegade's father taught his son 'never to trust the English' (p. 153).

4. Consider the following passage from Wolseley's *The Soldier's Pocketbook* which John Hobson quotes in his *The Psychology of Jingoism* (London: Grant Richards, 1901): 'As a nation we are brought up to feel it a disgrace to succeed by falsehood; the word "spy" conveys in it something as repulsive as slave. We will keep hammering away with the conviction that honesty is the best policy, and that truth always wins in the long run. These pretty little sentences do well for a child's copybook, but the man who acts upon them in war had better sheathe his sword forever' (p. 60).

5. See Ransford, *The Battle of Majuba Hill*, pp. 15–16, and Donald R. Morris, *The Washing of the Spears*, p. 446.

3. Some talk of Alexander: the imperial hero

1. See Frederick Garber's 'Self, Society, Value, and the Romantic Hero', in Victor Brombert, ed., *The Hero in Literature* (Greenwich, Conn.: Fawcett, 1969), pp. 213–27.
2. Haggard's descriptions of battle are more strikingly inadequate when compared with, say, Stephen Crane's descriptions of battle in *The Red Badge of Courage* (1895). The following passages from Crane's book underscore the weaknesses of Haggard's own writing:

> There was a singular absence of heroic poses. The men bending and surging in their haste and rage were in every impossible attitude. The steel ramrods clanked and clanged with incessant din as the men pounded them furiously into the hot rifle barrels. The flaps of the cartridge boxes were all unfastened, and bobbed idiotically with each movement. The rifles, once loaded, were jerked to the shoulder and fired without apparent aim into the smoke or at one of the blurred and shifting forms which upon the field before the regiment had been growing larger and larger like puppets under a magician's hand.
>
> The officers, at their intervals, rearward, neglected to stand in picturesque attitudes. They were bobbing to and fro roaring directions and encouragements. The dimensions of their howls were extraordinary. They expended their lungs with prodigal wills. And often they nearly stood upon their heads in their anxiety to observe the enemy on the other side of the tumbling smoke, *The Red Badge of Courage*, eds. Sculley Bradley, Richmond Croom Beatty, and E. Hudson Long, 2nd edn (New York: Norton, 1976), p. 32.
>
> It seemed to the youth that he saw everything. Each blade of the green grass was bold and clear. He thought that he was aware of every change in the thin, transparent vapour that floated idly in sheets. The brown or gray trunks of the trees showed each roughness of their surfaces. And the men of the regiment with their starting eyes and sweating faces, running madly, or falling, as if thrown headlong, to queer, heaped-up corpses – all were comprehended. His mind took a mechanical but firm impression, so that afterward everything was pictured and explained to him, save why he himself was there.
>
> But there was a frenzy made from this furious rush. The men, pitching forward insanely, had burst into cheerings, moblike and barbaric, but tuned in strange keys that can arouse the dullard and

the stoic. It made a mad enthusiasm that, it seemed, would be incapable of checking itself before granite and brass. There was the delirium that encounters despair and death, and is heedless and blind to the odds. It is a temporary but sublime absence of selfishness. And because it was of this order was the reason, perhaps, why the youth wondered, afterward, what reasons he could have had for being there. (p. 87)

3. In Bentley's view, 'If Hitler himself is indebted to literature it is more probably to the paranoic wild-west stories of Karl May, known to every German lad of his generation, than to the rather advanced thought of Carlyle and Nietzsche', *A Century of Hero-Worship*, 2nd edn (Boston: Beacon Hill Press, 1957), p. 253.

4. An intelligible order: Haggard's fatalism

1. This phrase is from his dedication to Henley in *Virginibus Puerisque* (1881): 'still the world appears a brave gymnasium, full of sea-bathing, and horse exercise, and bracing, manly virtues' (London: Chatto and Windus, 1911), p. vi.
2. See *Cetywayo, passim*.
3. See Jerome Hamilton Buckley's discussion of Henley's 'Pro Rege Nostro' and *The Song of the Sword* in his *William Ernest Henley* for another example of 'divine selection', or what Buckley calls 'a naive and misapplied Darwinism' (Princeton University Press, 1945), p. 137. Buckley finds the implications of England's being 'Spouse-in-Chief of the ancient Sword' ('Pro Rege Nostro') incomprehensible: 'Insofar as the Sword was aboriginally the prerequisite factor in the nation's survival, the Sword became, by Henleyean logic, the symbol of all cultural advance, and consequently, a good in itself . . . The Sword is the nisus of the evolutionary process, the great natural selector, the Will of God' (pp. 137–8).

5. Jekyll and Hyde abroad: science and spiritualism

1. For a fuller discussion of the relationship between imperialism and the natural sciences, see Gollwitzer's *Europe in the Age of Imperialism*, trans. David Adam and Stanley Baron (London: Thames and Hudson, 1969), pp. 19–30. Gollwitzer notes inventions in transport and advances in science that ushered in, for example, the first hydroelectric locomotive, the first electric power plant, the first hydroelectric generating station, the telephone, the wireless, and the incandescent bulb. Refrigeration techniques and canning, he writes, made possible the transportation of perishables to Europe from distant places; and there was also 'the invention of the machine-gun in 1883, the introduction of heavy weapons and armoured battleships, [and] the first designs for submarines and tanks' (p. 30).

6. 'A negro excepted': racism

1. According to E. A. Ritter's *Shaka Zulu* (London: Longmans, 1965), Shaka has been falsely accused of having killed his mother. Ritter claims that Shaka was sixty miles away from his mother's kraal when she lay critically ill from dysentery (p. 310). Whether or not Haggard knew this is uncertain. Ritter also offers a description of the horrible mourning rites observed by about 60,000 Zulus, roughly 7,000 of whom died in an indiscriminate massacre (p. 312). This description, similar to the one given by Donald R. Morris in *The Washing of the Spears*, resembles Haggard's own account of the mourning rites in *Nada*.

2. See Morris, *The Washing of the Spears*, pp. 67, 117; and E. A. Ritter, *Shaka Zulu*, pp. 314–27, 339.

BIBLIOGRAPHY

Since the following bibliography lists the actual texts used and not necessarily the first edition of those texts, it is not always possible to enter the works of Haggard and others in the chronological sequence in which they were published. However, when necessary the original date of publication is provided in parentheses at the end of the citation. In addition, within the body of the book itself I have endeavoured to note the original date of publication the first time each work is mentioned and afterwards if required by the context. Further bibliographical entries on Haggard may be found in J. E. Scott's *A Bibliography of the Works of Sir Henry Rider Haggard 1856–1925* and in the critical biographies of Haggard by Morton Cohen and D. S. Higgins cited below.

Unpublished materials

Columbia Collection. H. Rider Haggard Papers. Rare Books and Manuscript Library. Columbia University.
Norfolk Record Office. Haggard's Diaries. MS 4694/1/I–XXII. These twenty-two holograph volumes were begun at the start of the war in 1914 and continued until 1925, the year of Haggard's death.

Works by H. Rider Haggard

Because Haggard's works have been divided into sections, some 'a' and 'b' dates may be in either the fiction or non-fiction lists. The entries for Haggard comprise only those of his works quoted within the text. Titles referred to in passing and not quoted are not included.

a. Fiction

1887b. *Dawn.* New York: Harper and Brothers (1884).
1887c. *The Witch's Head.* New York: Harper and Brothers (1884).
[1888]. *Colonel Quaritch, V.C.* New York: P. F. Collier and Son.
[1889a]. *Jess.* New York: Worthington (1887).
1889b. *Cleopatra.* London: Longmans, Green.
1891. *Eric Brighteyes.* London: Longmans, Green.

1892a. *Nada the Lily*. New York: Longmans, Green.

1892b. *Beatrice*. London: Longmans, Green (1890).

1893. *Allan's Wife and Other Tales* (including 'A Tale of Three Lions'). London: Griffith, Farran (1889).

1894. *The People of the Mist*. London: Longmans, Green.

1898. *Dr Therne*. London: Longmans, Green.

1903. *Pearl Maiden*. London: Longmans, Green.

1904. *Stella Fregelius*. New York: Longmans, Green.

1905. *Ayesha*. New York: Doubleday, Page.

1906. *The Way of the Spirit*. London: Hutchinson.

1908. *The Ghost Kings*. London: Cassell.

1909. *The Yellow God*. London: Cassell.

1912. *Marie*. London: Cassell.

1919a. *Allan Quatermain*. London: Hodder and Stoughton (1887).

1919b. *When the World Shook*. London: Cassell.

1920. *The Ancient Allan*. New York: McKinlay, Stone and Mackenzie.

[1921]. *She and Allan*. London: Hutchinson.

1923. *Wisdom's Daughter*. London: Hutchinson.

[1924]. *Heu-Heu, or the Monster*. New York: Grossett and Dunlap.

1926b. *Treasure of the Lake*. New York: Doubleday, Page.

1952. *Child of Storm*. London: Macdonald (1913).

1955. *King Solomon's Mines*. London: Collins (1885).

1957. *She*. London: Collins (1887).

1962. *Finished*. London: Macdonald (1917).

1965a. *Benita*. London: Macdonald (1906).

1965b. *Queen Sheba's Ring*. London: Macdonald (1910).

1972. *The World's Desire* (in collaboration with Andrew Lang). New York: Ballantine Books (1890).

1981. 'Smith and the Pharaohs'. In *The Best Short Stories of Rider Haggard*, ed. Peter Haining. London: Michael Joseph (*Strand Magazine*, 1913).

b. Non-fiction

1877a. 'A Zulu War Dance'. *Gentleman's Magazine*, CCXLIII, pp. 94–107.

1877b. 'The Transvaal'. *Macmillan's Magazine*, XXXVI, pp. 71–9.

1877c. 'A visit to the Chief Secocoeni'. *Gentleman's Magazine*, CCXLIII, pp. 302–18.

1887a. 'About fiction'. *Contemporary Review*, LI, pp. 172–80.

1896. *Cetywayo and His White Neighbours*. 2nd edn. London: Kegan Paul, Trench, Trübner (1882).

1902. *Rural England*. 2 vols. London: Longmans, Green.

1916. *The After-War Settlement and the Employment of Ex-Service Men in the Overseas Dominions*. Report to the Royal Colonial Institute. London: The Saint Catherine Press for the Royal Colonial Institute.

Bibliography

1926a. *The Days of My Life.* Ed. C. J. Longman. 2 vols. London: Longmans, Green.

c. Letters to The Times

6 November 1893, 'The New Sentiment', p. 8.
16 August 1913, 'Umslopogaas and Makokel', p. 5.
10 October 1914, 'The Death of Mark Haggard', p. 9.
7 February 1920, 'Air Exploration and Empire', p. 8.
3 March 1920, 'The Liberty League', p. 12.
31 March 1922, 'Boy Emigration', p. 8.
1 May 1923, 'Liberalism and Land Reform', p. 15.

Other works cited in the text

a. Books and parts of books

Arendt, Hannah. 1958. *The Origins of Totalitarianism.* 2nd edn. Cleveland: World (1951).

Auerbach, Nina. 1982. *Woman and the Demon.* Cambridge: Harvard University Press.

Bentley, Eric. 1957. *A Century of Hero-Worship.* 2nd edn. Boston: Beacon Hill Press (1944).

Bowra, C. M. 1964. 'The meaning of a heroic age'. In *The Language and Background of Homer.* Selected and introduced by G. S. Kirk, pp. 22–47. Cambridge: W. Heffer (1957).

Buchan, John. 1910. *Prester John.* Boston: Houghton Mifflin.

Buckley, Jerome Hamilton. 1945. *William Ernest Henley, A Study in 'Counter Decadence' of the Nineties.* Princeton University Press.

Bursey, Wallace. 1972. 'Rider Haggard: a study in popular fiction'. Diss. Memorial University of Newfoundland.

Carrington, Charles E. 1970. *Rudyard Kipling, His Life and Work.* Harmondsworth, Middlesex: Pelican (1955).

Chase, Richard. 1969. 'Novel vs. romance'. In *Pastoral and Romance,* ed. Eleanor Terry Lincoln, pp. 282–8. Englewood Cliffs, N.J.: Prentice-Hall (1957).

Cohen, Morton. 1968. *Rider Haggard, His Life and Work.* 2nd edn. London: Macmillan (1960).

Cohen, Morton, ed. 1965. *Rudyard Kipling to Rider Haggard, The Record of a Friendship.* London: Hutchinson.

Crane, Stephen. 1976. *The Red Badge of Courage.* Ed. Sculley Bradley, Richmond Croom Beatty, and E. Hudson Long. New York: Norton (1895).

Crankshaw, Edward. 1952. *The Forsaken Idea, A Study of Viscount Milner.* London: Longmans, Green.

Daiches, David. 1969. *Some Late Victorian Attitudes*. London: André Deutsch.

Darton, Harvey. 1966. *Children's Books in England*. 2nd edn. Cambridge University Press (1932).

Dilke, Charles Wentworth. 1869. *Greater Britain*. 2 vols. in one. Philadelphia: Lippincott.

Doyle, Arthur Conan. 1912. *The Lost World*. Toronto: Musson.

Eigner, Edwin M. 1964. *Robert Louis Stevenson and the Romantic Tradition*. Princeton University Press.

Eliot, T. S. 1964. *The Sacred Wood*. 2nd edn. London: Methuen (1920).

Eliot, T. S., ed. 1963. *A Choice of Kipling's Verse*. London: Faber and Faber (1941).

Ellis, Peter Berresford. 1978. *H. Rider Haggard, A Voice from the Infinite*. London: Routledge and Kegan Paul.

Elwin, Malcolm. 1939. *Old Gods Falling*. New York: Macmillan.

Ensor, R. C. K. 1936. *England, 1870–1914*. Oxford University Press.

Etherington, Norman. 1984. *Rider Haggard*. Boston, Twayne.

Frye, Northrop. 1957. *Anatomy of Criticism*. Princeton University Press.

Garber, Frederick. 1969. 'Self, society, value, and the romantic hero'. In *The Hero in Literature*, ed. Victor Brombert, pp. 213–27. Greenwich, Connecticut: Fawcett.

Gerould, Gordon Hall. 1942. *The Patterns of English and American Fiction*. Boston: Little, Brown.

Gollwitzer, Heinz. 1969. *Europe in the Age of Imperialism, 1880–1914*. Trans. David Adam and Stanley Baron. London: Thames and Hudson.

Grahame, Kenneth. 1961. *The Wind in the Willows*. London: Methuen (1908).

Gray, Herbert Branston. 1913. *The Public Schools and the Empire*. London: Williams and Northgate.

Green, Roger Lancelyn. 1946. *Andrew Lang, A Critical Biography*. Leicester: Edmund Ward.

Greene, Graham. 1951. *The Lost Childhood and Other Essays*. London: Eyre and Spottiswoode.

Haggard, Lilias Rider. 1951. *The Cloak That I Left*. London: Hodder and Stoughton.

Halévy, Elie. 1926. *Imperialism and the Rise of Labour*. Trans. E. I. Watkin. London: Ernest Benn.

Henley, William Ernest, ed. 1921a. *Lyra Heroica, A Book of Verse for Boys*. London: Macmillan (1892).

Henley, William Ernest. 1921b. *Poems*. London: Macmillan.
1926. *Poems*. New York: Scribner's.

Higgins, D. S. 1983. *Rider Haggard, A Biography*. New York: Stein and Day.

Higgins, D. S., ed. 1980. *The Private Diaries of Sir H. Rider Haggard 1914–1925*. London: Cassell.

Bibliography

Hobhouse, L. T. 1904. *Democracy and Reaction.* London: Unwin.

Hobman, D. L. 1955. *Olive Schreiner, Her Friends and Times.* London: Watts.

Hobson, John A. 1901. *The Psychology of Jingoism.* London: Grant Richards.
  1965. *Imperialism, A Study.* Rev. edn. Ann Arbor: University of Michigan Press (1902).

Housman, A. E. 1923. *A Shropshire Lad.* London: Grant Richards (1896).

Hughes, H. Stuart. 1958. *Consciousness and Society, The Reorientation of European Social Thought 1890–1930.* New York: Knopf.

Hynes, Samuel. 1972. *Edwardian Occasions.* London: Routledge and Kegan Paul.

'Imperialist' [pseud. for James Rochfort Maguire]. 1897. *Cecil Rhodes, A Biography and an Appreciation, With Personal Reminiscences by Dr. Jameson.* London: Macmillan.

James, Henry. 1968. 'The art of fiction'. In *The Portable Henry James*, ed. Morton Dauwen Zabel, pp. 387–414. Rev. edn. New York: Viking (1884).
  1970. Preface to *The American.* In *The Novels and Tales of Henry James*, vol. II, pp. v–xxiii. New York edn. New York: Augustus M. Kelley (1907).

Kipling, Rudyard. 1897. *The Jungle Book.* New York: Charles Scribner's Sons (1894).
  1904. *Traffics and Discoveries.* Toronto: Morang.
  1919. *Rudyard Kipling's Verse, 1885–1918.* New York: Doubleday, Page.
  1967. *Kim.* London: Macmillan (1901).

Lang, Andrew. 1891. *Essays in Little.* New York: Charles Scribner's Sons.
  1892. *Letters on Literature.* London: Longmans, Green.

Lehmann, Joseph. 1972. *The First Boer War.* London: Jonathan Cape.

LeMay, G. H. L. 1965. *British Supremacy in South Africa, 1899–1907.* Oxford: Clarendon.

Maguire, James Rochfort. See 'Imperialist'.

Masterman, C. F. G. 1901. *The Heart of the Empire.* London: T. Fisher Unwin.

Milner, Lord Alfred. 1913. *The Nation and the Empire.* London: Constable.

Morris, Donald R. 1966. *The Washing of the Spears.* London: Jonathan Cape.

Newbolt, Henry. 1919. *Poems: New and Old.* Toronto: McClelland and Stewart.

Nordan, Pierre. 1966. *Conan Doyle.* Trans. Frances Partridge. London: John Murray.

Osbourne, Lloyd. 1924. *An Intimate Portrait of Robert Louis Stevenson.* New York: Charles Scribner's Sons.

Praz, Mario. 1970a. *The Hero in Eclipse in Victorian Fiction.* Trans. Angus Davidson. 2nd edn. London: Oxford University Press (1956).
  1970b. *The Romantic Agony.* Trans. Angus Davidson. 2nd edn. London: Oxford University Press (1933).

Ransford, Oliver. 1967. *The Battle of Majuba Hill.* London: John Murray.

Bibliography

Raymond, E. T. [pseud. for Edward Raymond Thompson]. 1923. *The Life of Lord Rosebery*. New York: George Doran.

Ritter, E. A. 1965. *Shaka Zulu*. London: Longmans.

Robinson, Ronald and John Gallagher. 1961. *Africa and the Victorians*. London: Macmillan.

Sandison, Alan. 1967. *The Wheel of Empire*. London: Macmillan.

Seeley, John. 1971. *The Expansion of England*, ed. John Gross. University of Chicago Press (1883).

Shanks, Edward. 1927. 'Rider Haggard and the novel of adventure'. In his *Second Essays on Literature*, pp. 126–41. London: Collins.

Stevenson, Robert Louis. 1910. *Master of Ballantrae, Weir of Hermiston, Poems*. New York: Scribner's (1889 [*Master*], 1896 [*Weir*]).

1911. *Virginibus Puerisque*. London: Chatto and Windus (1881).

1924. *The Letters of Robert Louis Stevenson*, ed. Sidney Colvin. Vol. IV. In *The Works of Robert Louis Stevenson*. Tusitala Edition. Vol. XXXIV. London: Heinemann.

1947. 'A humble remonstrance'. In *Selected Writings of Robert Louis Stevenson*, ed. Saxe Cummins. New York: Modern Library (1884).

1968. *Dr. Jekyll and Mr. Hyde*. London: Dent (1886).

1969. *Treasure Island*. London: Pan (1883).

Stokes, Eric. 1972. 'Kipling's imperialism'. In *Rudyard Kipling, the Man, his Work and his World*, ed. John Gross, pp. 89–98. London: Weidenfeld and Nicolson.

Thompson, Edward Raymond. See Raymond, E. T.

Thornton, William. 1965. *Doctrines of Imperialism*. New York: John Wiley.

Walker, Eric A. 1965. *A History of Southern Africa*. 3rd edn. London: Longmans.

Wallace, Edgar. 1933. *Sanders of the River*. London: Ward, Lock (1911).

Wells, H. G. 1946. *The New Machiavelli*. Harmondsworth, Middlesex: Penguin (1911).

b. Articles and miscellaneous reviews

Anonymous reviews have been entered by title when possible, with the book under review identified later in the same item.

Athenaeum. 31 October 1885. Review of *King Solomon's Mines*. LXXXVI, p. 568.

10 January 1885. Review of *The Witch's Head*. LXXXV. p. 49.

Brown, Ivor. 26 March 1961. 'Tales of a teller'. Review of *Rider Haggard, His Life and Work*. *New York Times Book Review*, CXI, pp. 5, 45.

Ellis, H. F. January 1959. 'The niceties of plagiarism'. *The Atlantic Monthly*, CCIII, pp. 76–8.

Henley, William Ernest. 1900. 'Concerning Atkins'. *Pall Mall Magazine*, XXI (May to August), pp. 280–3.

Hutchinson, Horace G. October 1926. 'Sir Rider Haggard's autobiography'. Review of *The Days of My Life. Edinburgh Review*, CCXLIV, pp. 343–55.

[Lang, Andrew]. 10 October 1885. Review of *King Solomon's Mines. Saturday Review*, LX, pp. 485–6.

Lewis, C. S. 3 September 1960. 'Haggard rides again'. *Time and Tide*, XLI, pp. 1044–5.

Literary World (London). 6 February 1885. Review of *The Witch's Head*. XXXI [N.S.], pp. 130–1.

'Mr. Rider Haggard on poverty'. 15 July 1911. *The Times*, p. 11.

'Novel notes'. November 1895. Review of *Joan Haste. Bookman* (New York), II, p. 229.

Porter, Peter. 'Viewpoint'. 7 July 1972. *The Times Literary Supplement*, p. 774.

Pritchett, V. S. 27 August 1960. 'Haggard still riding'. *New Statesman*, LX, pp. 277–8.

'Reality and romance'. 28 April 1888. *Spectator*, LXI, pp. 569–71.

Saintsbury, George. 17 January 1885. Review of *The Witch's Head. Academy*, XXVII, p. 41.

Saturday Review. 17 January 1885. Review of *The Witch's Head*. LIX, pp. 84–5.

'The Wheat and the Chaff'. 11 April 1958. Review of *King Solomon's Mines. The Times Literary Supplement*, p. xxii.

INDEX

Index

Index